MACMILLAN FIELD GUIDES

Birds
of
North America

WESTERN REGION

A Quick Identification Guide
for All Bird-Watchers

by

John Bull and Edith Bull
Illustrated by James Coe

COLLIER BOOKS
Macmillan Publishing Company, New York
Collier Macmillan Publishers, London

Collier Books
Macmillan Publishing Company
866 Third Avenue, New York, NY 10022
Collier Macmillan Canada, Inc.

Library of Congress Cataloging-in-Publication Data
Bull, John L.
    Birds of North America. Western region: a quick identification guide to common
birds/by John Bull and Edith Bull; illustrated by James Coe.—1st Collier Books ed.
    p.   cm.—(Macmillan field guides)
Includes index.
ISBN 0-02-062580-4
1. Birds—West (U.S.)—Identification.   2. Birds—North America—Identification.
I. Bull, Edith.   II. Title.   III. Series.
QL683.W4B85 1989b
598.2978—dc20   89-31875   CIP

Macmillan books are available at special discounts for bulk purchases for sales
promotions, premiums, fund-raising, or educational use. For details, contact:

Special Sales Director
Macmillan Publishing Company
866 Third Avenue
New York, NY 10022

10 9 8 7 6 5 4 3 2 1

First Collier Books Edition 1989

Printed in the United States of America

Contents

Acknowledgments

We wish to thank both Guy Tudor and John Yrizarry for their many helpful suggestions in reference to the color plates. We are greatly indebted to the scientific staff of the Ornithology Department, American Museum of Natural History, for use of the unparalleled collections there. In addition, James Coe would like to thank his family for their encouragement and unwavering support. Finally, we also thank our editor, Elisa Petrini, for her valued assistance, patience, and indugence.

John Bull
Edith Bull
James Coe

Introduction:
How to Use This Book

This is a book about identifying birds and how to identify them easily. It has a unique format that will help even beginners learn to recognize species quickly. Rather than present birds in scientific categories, we group them according to similarity of color, pattern, behavior, or habitat. We thus have, for example, Reddish Birds, Bluish Birds, Tree Clingers, Woodpeckers, Flycatchers, Swallows, Grassland Birds, and Shorebirds. The text accompanying each color plate—indeed, each species—emphasizes simply and quickly the salient features, the so-called field marks, that enable you to sort out a particular bird almost instantly. You will find that certain field marks appear in italics—these are the critical distinguishing marks of particular species.

For easy reference, we have also arranged the birds according to their abundance. Most bird guides follow a strict phylogenetic, or evolutionary, order in presenting the birds, beginning with the supposedly most primitive types—the loons and grebes—and ending with the most advanced—the finches and sparrows. In other words, they start with the water birds and finish with the land birds. In this volume, we reverse the sequence, starting with the more familiar land birds of yard, garden, field, and park, such as the blackbirds, sparrows, thrushes, and warblers. We end with the somewhat less familiar aquatic types, such as the ducks, gulls, and herons.

Further, to minimize confusion, we have chosen to focus on the most common and conspicuous species rather than on the 700 or so that are found in the Western United States. There are 340 species illustrated in the 54 plates. Some of the birds included are common throughout the West, some in specific regions of the West, others in rather small areas of the West. No rare birds are depicted, but some species are uncommon in various regions, while abundant elsewhere. The Roadrunner, for example, is commonly seen in parts of the Southwest, especially Arizona, but rarely ventures as far northeast as Kansas. For our purposes, Western North America stretches from southern Canada (50° N) to the Mexican border, and from the Pacific coast to the Dakotas and the southernmost Gulf coast of Texas (see map). The dividing line begins on the eastern borders of North and South Dakota, Nebraska, Kansas, and Oklahoma, and includes most of Texas, excepting much of the southeastern portion.

The color plates are, in most instances, designed to group birds according to appearance, even when the birds are not scientifically related. The fact is that many birds, though widely separated by evolution, often look remarkably alike, especially to the novice. We call them "unrelated look-alikes."

To keep the book as straightforward as possible, we show the outstanding colors and patterns for each species. When males and females differ greatly in appearance, both are shown, or the differences are mentioned in the text opposite the plate. Males *usually* have more distinctive plumage than females, both as to color and pattern, so we have depicted more males. On Plate 26, "Hummingbirds," for example, we show eight males with outstanding markings. Their female counterparts are somewhat drab and, if depicted, would look confusingly similar. Thus only one female, the Black-chinned Hummingbird—a common and widespread species—is shown in flight, hovering in front of a flower.

In other cases—for example, among the vast number of water birds—the sexes are virtually identical or similar in plumage. For these birds, only one figure per species is illustrated.

We have tried to depict birds in natural positions and settings, while emphasizing their distinguishing markings. For example, most waterfowl are shown only in the water or when they are perched. Flying birds are kept to a minimum—most ducks are more difficult to identify in flight. Certain exceptions include the Willet, which reveals its distinctive black and white wing pattern only while in flight, not when at rest. Hawks, by contrast, *are* depicted in flight, to emphasize their distinctive underwing markings and because their body and tail patterns, their shape, and their flight behavior are important factors in identification.

To keep bird identification as easy as possible, the descriptions opposite each plate have been pared to the absolute essentials. You will find that many of the details in the paintings are not mentioned in the descriptive material opposite the plates. The text highlights only those field marks that distinguish a particular bird from all others.

No attempt is made to describe bird songs, but for those few whose call is familiar, that fact is mentioned.

The plates that follow may be used without further comments, except one: You do need to know roughly what group of birds you're looking for. Is it a duck or a gull? A finch or a warbler? Chapter II provides added information to these groupings, making it easier to use the plates.

You may say that of course you know the difference between a duck and a gull. Fine, that's a good start. But what about the difference between a duck and a goose? A bluebird and a Blue Jay? Or a Blue Jay and a Belted Kingfisher? Knowing such differences—or at least appreciating the fact that they exist—is the first step in identifying what you see.

For example: The Belted Kingfisher is always found near water, for it feeds only on small fish; you will not find this bird in the middle of a forest or in a desert or anywhere far from water. It has a very large, shaggy head, which makes it look top-heavy. It is possible, however, for the beginner to confuse it with the Blue Jay, because both birds have a generally blue-white appearance and both have crests. But the Blue Jay's head does not have the outsized appearance, and the Blue Jay is smaller than the Belted Kingfisher. Further, the Belted Kingfisher dives into the water for its food, something the Blue Jay never does.

Take another example—obvious, perhaps, but basic: Most ducks don't roost in trees; they are usually (although not always) found on the ground or in the water. Thus, if you saw a rather large bird perched in a tree, the chances are good that it wouldn't be a duck. This is identification by elimination. Identification is made easier by knowing immediately what a bird cannot be.

The bird world is divided into water birds and land birds, although many of each are often found in the other's habitat.

Water birds include swans, geese, ducks, and other duck-like birds, generally described as waterfowl. Water birds also include such wading birds as herons and egrets. Finally, water birds encompass shorebirds such as plovers and sandpipers, gulls and terns.

The land birds take in everything else—the birds we see in woods, fields, yards, gardens, parks, farms, villages, and city streets: the hawks, owls, pigeons, sparrows, woodpeckers, warblers, finches, and so on.

Before you do any birding, we suggest that you read the material opposite the plates. It will simplify the process of learning to identify birds. There is also much additional information in Chapter II, "Further Comments on Plates."

I. Plate Descriptions

Just before the color plates you will find black and white figures describing bird topography or field marks, as well as some examples of wings, tails, bills, and feet. Together with other physical features, such as crests, and the various patterns and colors of the plumage, they form what are known as field marks. The following summary of the black and white plates on pages 5 to 7 contains an example of each type of anatomical feature.

Familiarize yourself with the examples illustrated and you will find that learning to distinguish the different birds will shortly become a relatively easy and fascinating pastime.

Facing each color plate is the description of the bird shown, enabling the reader to identify it. All the important characteristics of size, shape, color, pattern, and—where relevant—behavior are indicated. No irrelevant or confusing detailed descriptions are included.

Following the section on field marks are two categories:

1. **Habitat**—Only those places are mentioned in which the bird in question may be found during the nesting season—usually in spring and summer or, if necessary, in fall and winter. Spring and fall migrations are normally excluded, since birds may turn up in many different habitats at those times. However, if the bird in question is found only during spring and/or fall, then the habitats are listed.

2. **Range**—It is most important for the observer to know *where* a bird is likely to occur. The endpaper maps show the area covered in this volume. For example, a few species live in a very restricted area, such as in the southern portion of Texas, Arizona, or California. At the other extreme, a large percentage of the birds included in this book are widespread in range, and this information is given—for example, "from s. Canada to the Mexican border."

Field Marks
(BODY CHARACTERISTICS)

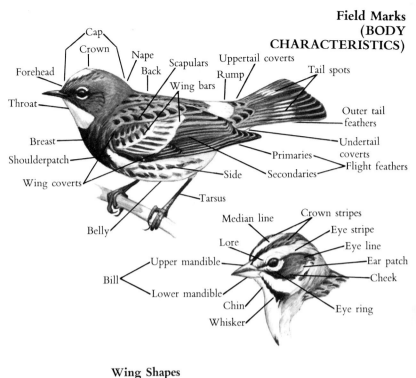

Cap
Crown
Nape
Scapulars
Forehead
Back
Wing bars
Throat
Breast
Shoulderpatch
Wing coverts
Belly
Tarsus
Side
Uppertail coverts
Rump
Tail spots
Outer tail feathers
Undertail coverts
Primaries
Flight feathers
Secondaries

Median line
Crown stripes
Eye stripe
Eye line
Ear patch
Lore
Cheek
Upper mandible
Bill
Lower mandible
Chin
Whisker
Eye ring

Wing Shapes

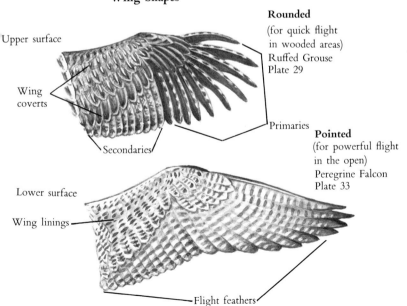

Upper surface

Wing coverts

Secondaries

Primaries

Rounded
(for quick flight
in wooded areas)
Ruffed Grouse
Plate 29

Pointed
(for powerful flight
in the open)
Peregrine Falcon
Plate 33

Lower surface

Wing linings

Flight feathers

5

Tail Shapes

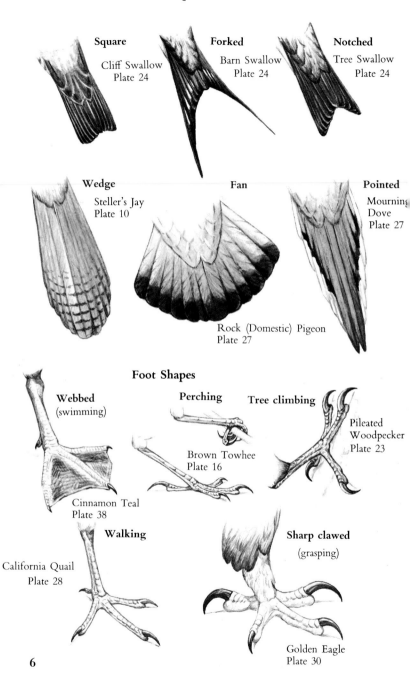

Square
Cliff Swallow
Plate 24

Forked
Barn Swallow
Plate 24

Notched
Tree Swallow
Plate 24

Wedge
Steller's Jay
Plate 10

Fan

Pointed
Mourning
Dove
Plate 27

Rock (Domestic) Pigeon
Plate 27

Foot Shapes

Webbed
(swimming)

Perching

Tree climbing
Pileated
Woodpecker
Plate 23

Brown Towhee
Plate 16

Cinnamon Teal
Plate 38

Walking

California Quail
Plate 28

Sharp clawed
(grasping)

Golden Eagle
Plate 30

Bill Shapes

Short, stout
(all-purpose)

Thin, pointed
(insect-eating)

Thick, conical
(seed-eating)

Scrub Jay
Plate 10

Orange-crowned
Warbler
Plate 4

Black-headed
Grosbeak
Plate 3

Flower probe

Short, wide-gaped
(aerial flycatching)

Chisel

Anna's
Hummingbird
Plate 26

Hairy Woodpecker
Plate 21

Poorwill
Plate 25

Spear

Earth probe

Great Blue Heron
Plate 46

Hooked

Common Snipe
Plate 49

Upturned

American Avocet
Plate 48

Swainson's Hawk
Plate 31

Spatulate

Downturned

Mallard
Plate 37

White-faced Ibis
Plate 47

7

KEY TO PLATE ABBREVIATIONS

Locations
c. = central
e. = eastern
n. = northern
s. = southern
w. = western
n.w. = northwestern
s.w. = southwestern
U.S. = United States

Plumages
ad. = adult
imm. = immature
F. = female
M. = male

Plate 1. REDDISH BIRDS

PURPLE FINCH — 6″
Washed with purplish-red; *unstreaked sides;* female—heavily streaked brown; white line behind eye; dark face patches. **Habitat:** Conifers, mixed woods; orchards, gardens, parks, yards; feeders. **Range:** Mainly Pacific Coast from s. Canada to Mexican border.

HOUSE FINCH — 5½″
Red forehead, eye line, throat, breast, and rump; *streaked sides;* whitish wing bars; female—heavily streaked brown; no facial pattern. **Habitat:** Conifers, mixed woods; dry scrub; ranches, farms; parks, suburbs, cities; feeders. **Range:** S. British Columbia to Mexican border, east to edge of Great Plains, south to Texas.

WHITE-WINGED CROSSBILL — 6½″
Bright pink; black tail and wings; two white wing bars; crossed bill at close range. **Habitat:** Conifers; winter—also mixed woods. **Range:** S. British Columbia, Alberta to Washington, Montana, n.w. Wyoming; in winter to Oregon, Utah, n. New Mexico.

RED CROSSBILL — 6″
Brick-red; blackish wings and tail; crossed bill at close range. **Habitat:** Conifers; winter—also mixed woods. **Range:** S. British Columbia, Alberta to Mexican border at higher elevations, east to edge of Great Plains; winters to n.w. Texas.

PINE GROSBEAK — 9″
Pinkish-red with gray sides and belly; blackish tail and wings; two white wing bars. **Habitat:** Conifers; winter—also mixed woods; orchards. **Range:** S. British Columbia, s.w. Alberta to mountains of c. California, n. Arizona, New Mexico; winters to n.w. Texas, n. Oklahoma.

ROSY FINCH — 6″
In most widespread form ("Gray-crowned")—black forehead; gray hind-crown; brown cheeks, back, throat, and breast; pinkish-rose rump, sides, and belly; pinkish wash on wings; yellow bill in winter. **Habitat:** High altitudes above tree line on bare ground and rocks, in short grass; winter— at lower elevations, mainly grassy fields, but often at feeders in severe weather. **Range:** Mountains from s. British Columbia, Alberta to c. California, n. Arizona, New Mexico; winters from w. portions of Dakotas to Kansas.

Plate 1. **REDDISH BIRDS**

Purple
Finch

F.

F.

M.

House
Finch

M.

White-winged
Crossbill

Red
Crossbill

Pine
Grosbeak

Rosy Finch
("Gray-crowned" race)

11

Plate 2. REDDISH/ORANGE BIRDS

NORTHERN ("BULLOCK'S") ORIOLE — 7½"
Black and bright orange; large white wing patch; black tail with orange patches; female—greenish-gray back; yellowish head and throat; grayish-white belly. **Habitat:** Open woods, river groves, roadside shade trees; farms, towns; occasionally at feeders. **Range:** S. Canada to Mexican border, east to edge of Great Plains; winters south of border.

HOODED ORIOLE — 7½"
Black and bright orange; orange crown and head; black face, throat, and chest; *all*-black tail. **Habitat:** Riverine trees, especially palms, willows, cottonwoods; scrub in arid areas; city parks, suburban hummingbird feeders. **Range:** C. portions of California, Nevada south to Mexican border, southeast to s. Texas; winters north to s. Arizona.

VERMILION FLYCATCHER — 6"
Flaming red crown and underparts; blackish-brown above. **Habitat:** Arid areas with scattered trees and shrubs near ponds and streams. **Range:** S. California, Arizona, New Mexico, w. and s. Texas; winters to just north of Mexican border.

SUMMER TANAGER — 7½"
Rose-red; *pale* bill. **Habitat:** Cottonwoods and willows along streams and near ponds. **Range:** S.w. U.S. north and east to c. California, s. Nevada, Utah, Texas, c. Oklahoma; winters south of Mexican border.

HEPATIC TANAGER — 7½"
Brick-red; grayish cheeks, *dark* bill; **Habitat:** Mixed pine-oak forests at higher elevations. **Range:** S. California, Arizona, New Mexico, w. Texas; winters mainly south of Mexican border.

PYRRHULOXIA — 8"
Gray with dark red crest, face, outer wings, and tail; rose-pink below from throat to center of belly; *yellow* bill. **Habitat:** Generally, dry open country with thickets, thorn scrub, hedgerows; ranches; feeders. **Range:** S. parts of Arizona, New Mexico; w. and s.c. Texas.

CARDINAL — 8½"
Bright *red,* including crest and bill; *black* face; female—similar, but light brown; only bill, tip of crest, wings, and tail are *red.* **Habitat:** Wooded edges, thickets, hedges; city parks, suburban gardens, yards; feeders; also desert scrub. **Range:** S.e. South Dakota south through Plains States to w. and s. Texas; s.w. U.S. from s. parts of New Mexico, Arizona to s. California (local).

Plate 2. **REDDISH/ORANGE BIRDS**

F.

M.

Northern
("Bullock's")
Oriole

Hooded
Oriole

Vermilion
Flycatcher

Summer
Tanager

Pyrrhuloxia

Hepatic
Tanager

F.

M.

Cardinal

13

Plate 3. YELLOWISH BIRDS

LESSER (DARK-BACKED) GOLDFINCH — 4″
Black crown, tail, and wings; white wing patch; green nape, back, and rump; yellow below; Black-backed form similar, but all black above. **Habitat:** Open brushy fields, wooded edges; farms, gardens; suburban feeders. **Range:** W. Oregon, California east to Colorado, New Mexico, s.w. Texas. "Green-backed" form occurs in w. parts, "Black-backed" in e. parts; rare in winter north to Utah, Colorado.

LAWRENCE'S GOLDFINCH — 4¼″
Black face, tail, and wings; *three* yellow wing patches; gray hindcrown, cheeks, back, and flanks; yellow rump and breast. **Habitat:** Dry, grassy hillsides; canyons with scattered trees and shrubs; fields; suburban feeders. **Range:** Local from n. California, c. Arizona to Mexican border.

AMERICAN GOLDFINCH — 5″
Bright yellow body; black forecrown, wings, and tail; female—mostly olive above, dull yellow below; black wings and tail. **Habitat:** Weedy fields; farms, orchards, gardens; city parks; suburban feeders. **Range:** S. Canada to Mexican border; in winter withdraws from n. portions.

PINE SISKIN — 5″
Heavily streaked; slender bill; small yellow patches on wings and tail. **Habitat:** Conifers in summer, bushy fields in winter; feeders. **Range:** S. Canada to Mexican border, but erratic and irregular in winter in South.

SCOTT'S ORIOLE — 8″
Black head, throat, breast, upper back, and tail; yellow rump, belly, bend of wing, and sides of tail. **Habitat:** Arid areas with yuccas, palms, pinyon-oak woods; occasionally at hummingbird feeders. **Range:** C. California, Nevada, Utah to Mexican border, s.e. to w. Texas; some winter in s. California, s.e. Arizona.

WESTERN TANAGER — 7″
Red head; black back, wings, and tail; yellow body; two wing bars—one yellow, one white. **Habitat:** Montane conifer forests in summer; migration—lowland deciduous woods and fruit trees. **Range:** S. British Columbia, Alberta to Mexican border, east to edge of Great Plains; winters south of border.

BLACK-HEADED GROSBEAK — 7½″
Black head, back, tail, and wings; two white wing bars; orange-brown collar, rump, breast, and sides; yellow belly. **Habitat:** Open mixed forests, wooded edges. **Range:** S. British Columbia, Alberta to Mexican border, east to Dakotas, Nebraska, Kansas; winters south of border.

EVENING GROSBEAK — 8″
Golden-yellow and dark brown; yellow forecrown and eye line; black tail and wings; large white wing patch; thick yellowish bill. **Habitat:** Conifers, mixed forests in summer; shade trees, city parks; suburban feeders. **Range:** S. British Columbia, Alberta to Mexican border, local in Southwest.

14

Lesser ("Dark-backed") race
Goldfinch

Plate 3. **YELLOWISH BIRDS**

Lawrence's
Goldfinch

Pine Siskin

F.

M.

American
Goldfinch

Scott's
Oriole

Western
Tanager

Black-
headed
Grosbeak

Evening
Grosbeak

15

Plate 4. YELLOWISH WARBLERS

VIRGINIA'S WARBLER — 4½"
Gray above; yellow rump; white eye ring; white below; yellow breast and vent; close range—rufous crown patch. **Habitat:** Montane areas with brush, pinyon-juniper woodland; yellow pine, spruce, fir. **Range:** E. Nevada, Utah, w. Colorado to s.e. California, Arizona, s.w. New Mexico, extreme w. Texas; winters south of border.

LUCY'S WARBLER — 4"
Gray above; rufous crown patch, rump; white below. **Habitat:** Desert mesquite; willows, cottonwoods along streams. **Range:** Mexican border to California, Nevada, Utah, Arizona, New Mexico; winters south of border.

NASHVILLE WARBLER — 4½"
Gray head; white eye ring; yellow below. **Habitat:** Open mixed woods; damp thickets; spruce-sphagnum bogs; parks, yards. **Range:** S. British Columbia, s.e. Manitoba; Washington, Idaho, w. Montana to c. California, Nevada, Utah; winters in s. California (local), and south of border.

ORANGE-CROWNED WARBLER — 5"
Olive-greenish above, yellowish below; grayish breast streaks close up; "orange" crown patch often hidden. **Habitat:** Brushy clearings; aspen, willow thickets; fields at forest borders. **Range:** S. Canada and U.S. from Pacific Coast east along Rockies to Mexican border; winters north to Oregon coast, inland to California, Arizona, s. Texas.

YELLOW WARBLER — 5"
Yellow, including wing bars; red breast streaks (male). **Habitat:** Willows, alders along streams; orchards, gardens, parks. **Range:** S. Canada to Mexican border; winters south of border, north to s. California, Arizona.

WILSON'S WARBLER — 5"
Black cap; yellow face and below. **Habitat:** Moist thickets, woodlands; gardens, parks, yards. **Range:** S. parts of British Columbia, Alberta; Washington, Idaho, w. Montana, in mountains to s. California, local to s. Arizona, New Mexico; winters south of border.

COMMON YELLOWTHROAT — 5"
Black mask; yellow throat and breast; female—lacks mask. **Habitat:** Moist thickets, marshes, fields; parks, gardens. **Range:** S. Canada to Mexican border; winters north to California, east to c. Texas.

MACGILLIVRAY'S WARBLER — 5¼"
Gray hood; black chest; partial white eye ring; yellow breast, belly. **Habitat:** Damp, shady thickets. **Range:** S. British Columbia, Alberta to c. California, east in mountains to w. New Mexico; winters south of border.

YELLOW-BREASTED CHAT — 7½"
Our largest warbler—olive-green above, white spectacles; yellow throat, breast; white belly. **Habitat:** Dense thickets, briars. **Range:** S. Canada to Mexican border; winters south of border, north to Texas.

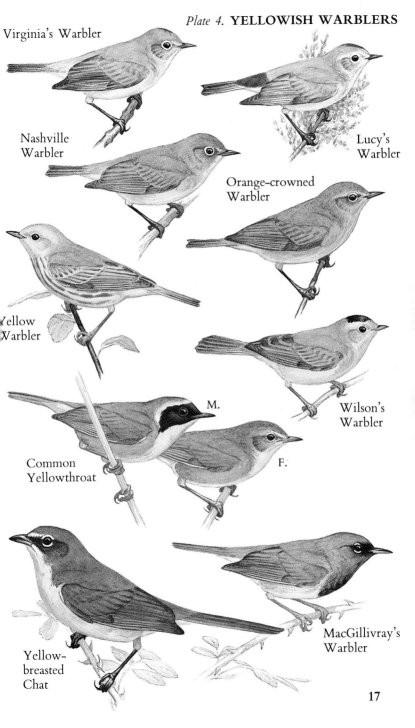

Plate 4. **YELLOWISH WARBLERS**

Virginia's Warbler

Nashville Warbler

Lucy's Warbler

Orange-crowned Warbler

Yellow Warbler

Wilson's Warbler

M.

F.

Common Yellowthroat

Yellow-breasted Chat

MacGillivray's Warbler

17

Plate 5. OTHER WARBLERS

HERMIT WARBLER — 4½″

Yellow head, black throat; gray back, tail, wings; two white wing bars; white breast, belly. **Habitat:** Montane conifer forests; migration—hardwoods. **Range:** Pacific Coast, interior mountains of s.w. Washington, Oregon, California; winters south of border, rarely to c. California.

GRACE'S WARBLER — 5″

Gray above; two white wing bars; yellow and white eye line; yellow throat and breast, white belly; black streaks along sides. **Habitat:** Montane pine, oak forests. **Range:** S. parts of Nevada, Utah, Colorado to Mexican border of Arizona, New Mexico; also extreme w. Texas; winters south of border.

TOWNSEND'S WARBLER — 5″

Black crown, cheek, throat; yellow line over and under cheek; yellow breast, black side stripes; two white wing bars. **Habitat:** Conifer forests; migration/winter—hardwoods. **Range:** S. British Columbia to Oregon, Idaho, c. Montana, w. Wyoming; migrates east to Great Plains; winters on coast of s. Oregon, California, and south of Mexican border.

BLACK-THROATED GRAY WARBLER — 5″

Like Townsend's Warbler, but yellow replaced by white. **Habitat:** Deciduous, mixed woods. **Range:** S. British Columbia, Idaho, Wyoming to Mexican border; winters north to s. California, s.w. Arizona.

YELLOW-RUMPED ("AUDUBON'S") WARBLER — 5¼″

Yellow rump, crown, throat, sides; black face and chest; gray back, tail, wings; white wing patch, breast, and belly; fall/winter—much duller, more brownish. **Habitat:** Conifer forests; migration/winter—mixed woodlands, thickets, gardens, parks. **Range:** S. Canada to Mexican border; winters north coast lowlands to British Columbia, inland to s.w. United States.

AMERICAN REDSTART — 5″

Black head and body; orange wing and tail patches; white belly; female—like male but with yellow patches; olive above, white below; gray head. **Habitat:** Open woodland; trees, shrubs. **Range:** S. Canada to Washington, Idaho, Utah, Colorado, e. Oklahoma; winters south of border, north to s. Texas.

PAINTED REDSTART — 5¼″

Black with scarlet breast; white wing and tail patches. **Habitat:** Montane hardwoods, especially oak; pine—often in canyons. **Range:** North to c. Arizona, s.w. New Mexico, w. Texas (Chisos Mountains); winters south of border, rarely in s. Arizona **Note:** Both redstarts flit about with spread wings and tail; frequently flycatching.

RED-FACED WARBLER — 5¼″

Scarlet face, throat, and chest; black cap and cheeks; white nape, rump, breast, and belly; gray back, wings, and tail. **Habitat:** Mountain forests. **Range:** North to e. Arizona, s.w. New Mexico; winters south of border.

18

Hermit Warbler

Plate 5. **OTHER WARBLERS**

Grace's
Warbler

Townsend's
Warbler

Black-throated
Gray Warbler

imm.
winter

ad.
summer

Yellow-rumped
("Audubon's")
Warbler

F.

M.

Red-faced
Warbler

American
Redstart

Painted
Redstart

19

Plate 6. GREENISH/GRAYISH BIRDS
(Kinglets, Vireos)

RUBY-CROWNED KINGLET — 4¼″

Tiny, short-tailed; white eye ring and wing bars; red crown patch (male only); olive above, grayish below. **Habitat:** Summer—conifers; migration/winter—mixed woodlands, thickets, shrubs. **Range:** S. British Columbia, Alberta, w. Montana through mountains to Mexican border; winters north to Oregon.

GOLDEN-CROWNED KINGLET — 4″

Tiny, short-tailed; black and white eye stripes; white wing bars; crown orange (male), yellow (female); olive above, grayish below. **Habitat:** Summer—conifers; migration/winter—mixed woodlands, thickets, shrubs. **Range:** S. Canada through mountains to Mexican border.

GRAY VIREO — 5″

Dull and nondescript—grayish above, paler below; narrow whitish eye ring and wing bar. **Habitat:** Dry scrub and pinyon-juniper thickets. **Range:** Mexican border north to s. parts of California, Nevada, Utah, Colorado, east to w. Texas (local); winters north to s. California, s. Arizona.

SOLITARY VIREO — 5″

White spectacles, wing bars, and underparts; gray head; gray back (West Coast); olive back (Rocky Mountains); dull greenish sides. **Habitat:** Open mixed forests; migration—suburban yards, city parks. **Range:** S. Canada through mountains to Mexican border; winters farther south.

WARBLING VIREO — 5″

Olive-gray above, white below; grayish eye stripe. **Habitat:** Open deciduous woodlands; aspen, poplar groves. **Range:** S. Canada to Mexican border; winters farther south.

RED-EYED VIREO — 6″

White eye stripe bordered by two black lines; gray crown; olive back, wings, and tail; whitish below; red eye at close range. **Habitat:** Woodlands, groves, shade trees. **Range:** S. parts of British Columbia east to Manitoba, but in U.S. mainly east of Rockies, south to Gulf of Mexico, local west to Washington, Montana, Colorado, Oklahoma; winters south of Mexican border.

Plate 6. **GREENISH/GRAYISH BIRDS (KINGLETS, VIREOS)**

Ruby-crowned Kinglet

Golden-crowned Kinglet

Gray Vireo

Solitary Vireo

Warbling Vireo

Red-eyed Vireo

21

Plate 7. **FLYCATCHERS**

WESTERN FLYCATCHER — 5½″

Olive-green above, yellowish below with olivaceous wash across breast; yellowish eye ring; two whitish wing bars. **Habitat:** Moist mixed forests; wooded suburbs, parks. **Range:** S. British Columbia, Alberta south through mountains and lowlands to Mexican border; winters farther south.

WESTERN WOOD PEWEE — 6½″

Drab; dull olive-gray above, paler below; two wing bars. **Habitat:** Open woodlands, shade trees. **Range:** S. Canada to Mexican border; winters farther south.

OLIVE-SIDED FLYCATCHER — 7½″

Stout; large head; short tail; olive-green above, dark sides below; yellowish center of breast and belly; at close range—white tufts on lower back. **Habitat:** Conifer forests in clearings, burns; perches at or near tops of tall trees with dead branches, stubs. **Range:** S. British Columbia, Alberta through mountains to California/Mexico border, c. parts of Arizona, New Mexico; winters south of border.

SAY'S PHOEBE — 7½″

Brownish-gray above; blackish tail; pale grayish-brown throat and breast; rusty-cinnamon belly; wags tail. **Habitat:** Deserts; plains with scrub; brushy canyons; ranches; perches on fences, rocks, low buildings. **Range:** S. Canada to Mexican border, east to w. portions of Dakotas, south to Texas; winters north to California, Arizona, New Mexico.

BLACK PHOEBE — 7″

Black with contrasting white belly; wags or pumps tail. **Habitat:** Open woodlands; shady streams; suburbs, parks; often nests near water. **Range:** N. California, s. Nevada, Utah, c. Arizona, New Mexico east to w. Texas, south to Mexican border.

ASH-THROATED FLYCATCHER — 8″

Gray-brown above; pale gray throat and breast; pale yellow belly; dusky tail with rufous webs; rufous wing edges. **Habitat:** Arid open country with scattered trees; deserts with mesquite; pinyon-juniper; other open woodlands. **Range:** S. parts of Washington, Idaho, Wyoming south to Mexican border, east to c. Texas; winters north to s. California, Arizona.

WESTERN KINGBIRD — 9″

Pale gray head, breast, and back—the back with olive wash; black mask, wings, and tail; white outer tail feathers; yellow belly. **Habitat:** Open country with scattered trees; roadside fences, wires. **Range:** S. Canada to Mexican border. Winters farther south.

EASTERN KINGBIRD — 8″

Black above, white below; broad white band at end of tail. **Habitat:** Farms, orchards; roadsides, fence posts, utility wires; lake and river shores. **Range:** S. Canada, east of Pacific Coast ranges, south to c. Nevada, Utah, n. New Mexico, c. Texas. Winters south of Mexican border.

Plate 7. **FLYCATCHERS**

Western Flycatcher

Olive-sided Flycatcher

Western Wood Pewee

Say's Phoebe

Ash-throated Flycatcher

Black Phoebe

Eastern Kingbird

Western Kingbird

23

Plate 8. LARGE GRAYISH BIRDS

TOWNSEND'S SOLITAIRE — 9″
Grayish body with dark wings and tail; whitish eye ring and outer tail feathers; buff wing patch; often perches upright. **Habitat:** Summer—mountain conifer forests; migration/winter—canyons, valleys with scrub and juniper thickets. **Range:** S. British Columbia, Alberta through mountains to Mexican border; at lower elevations in winter.

SCISSOR-TAILED FLYCATCHER — 13″
Extremely long black and white scissor-shaped tail; pale grayish-white body; bright salmon-pink wing linings, flanks, belly, and vent. **Habitat:** Open country—ranches; thickets; roadsides. **Range:** Texas, Oklahoma, Kansas north to s. Nebraska, west to e. Colorado, New Mexico, east to w. Missouri, Arkansas, Louisiana; winters south of border.

LOGGERHEAD SHRIKE — 9″
Black mask, wings, and tail; gray above, white below; hooked bill. **Habitat:** Open country with scattered trees, thorn scrub; cactus deserts; roadside barbed-wire fences. **Range:** Washington, s. parts of Alberta, Saskatchewan, Manitoba to Mexican border; winters north to c. states.

NORTHERN MOCKINGBIRD — 10½″
Pale gray above, whitish below; long tail; large white wing tail patches, most evident in flight. **Habitat:** Open country—deserts; ranches, fences, wires; parks, yards, gardens. **Range:** California east to Dakotas, north to s. Canada; south to Mexican border.

GRAY CATBIRD — 9″
Dark gray, black cap. **Habitat:** Shrubbery in parks, yards; dense thickets. **Range:** From s. Canada southeast through Montana, Wyoming, Dakotas, Nebraska, n.e. Kansas; winters from s. Texas south through Mexico.

DIPPER — 8″
Chunky, stub-tailed; slate-gray; bobs up and down. **Habitat:** Mountain streams with rocks; mainly aquatic, often submerging and feeding along pebbly stream bottoms. **Range:** S. British Columbia, Alberta, w. Montana, in mountains to Mexican border; lower elevations in winter.

CLARK'S NUTCRACKER — 12½″
Chunky, short-tailed; gray head and body; black wings and tail with large white patches. **Habitat:** High mountains in conifer forests up to tree line—often seen perched on dead snags; visits campsites, feeders. **Range:** S. British Columbia, Alberta, in high mountains to c. California, s. Arizona, New Mexico; lower elevations in winter.

GRAY JAY — 11½″
Gray back, wings, and tail; paler below; whitish head with black nape (Rocky Mountains) or black hindcrown (Pacific Coast ranges). **Habitat:** Chiefly dense conifer forests; visits campsites, feeders. **Range:** S. British Columbia, Alberta, in mountains along Pacific Coast to n. California and in Rockies to n. Arizona, New Mexico; also South Dakota (Black Hills).

24

Plate 8. **LARGE GRAYISH BIRDS**

Townsend's
Solitaire

Scissor-tailed
Flycatcher

Loggerhead
Shrike

Northern
Mockingbird

Dipper

Gray
Catbird

Clark's
Nutcracker

Gray
Jay

25

Plate 9. SMALL GRAYISH BIRDS
(Gnatcatchers, Tits)

BLACK-TAILED GNATCATCHER — 4½"
Black cap and tail; gray back, rump, and wings; white eye ring; whitish below. **Habitat:** Desert scrub, arid gullies with sage, mesquite, creosote. **Range:** S. California, Nevada, Arizona, New Mexico, w. and s. Texas.

BLUE-GRAY GNATCATCHER — 4½"
Blue-gray above, white below; long black tail with white edges; white eye ring. **Habitat:** Open mixed woods, near streams; thickets, chaparral in dry country; yards, parks. **Range:** N. California to e. Nebraska, south to Mexican border; winters from California to Texas and south.

BUSHTIT — 4"
Tiny, long-tailed; dull gray above, paler below; light brown cap (Pacific Coast); same color on face (interior); some have black mask—"Black-eared" form—(Mexican border from Arizona to Texas); male—dark eye; female—light eye. **Habitat:** Woods, pinyon-juniper, oak, chaparral. **Range:** S.w. British Columbia to Mexican border; inland from Washington, Idaho southeast to Colorado, w. Oklahoma, w. Texas.

VERDIN (YELLOW-HEADED TIT) — 4¼"
Gray above, whitish below; *yellow head;* chestnut shoulder patch. **Habitat:** Deserts—mesquite, creosote; hummingbird feeders. **Range:** S. California, Nevada, Utah, Arizona, New Mexico, w. Texas to Lower Gulf Coast.

PLAIN TITMOUSE — 5½"
Drab gray (inland), grayish-brown (Pacific Coast); crest. **Habitat:** Mixed woods, pinyon-juniper; parks; yards, feeders. **Range:** N. California east to Colorado, south to Mexican border; local in w. Texas.

BRIDLED TITMOUSE — 4½"
Gray, black-tipped crest; black and white face, black throat. **Habitat:** Oak, sycamore, pine woodlands; willow, cottonwood, mesquite in winter; feeders. **Range:** Mexico north to c. Arizona, s.w. New Mexico.

CHESTNUT-BACKED CHICKADEE — 5"
Blackish-brown cap; white cheeks; black throat; chestnut back, sides; white below. **Habitat:** Conifers; oak, eucalyptus groves; feeders. **Range:** Mainly Pacific Coast from s. British Columbia to c. California.

BLACK-CAPPED CHICKADEE — 5¼"
Black cap and throat; white cheeks and below; gray back, wings, tail. **Habitat:** Mixed woods, willow thickets; parks, yards; feeders. **Range:** S. Canada to n.w. California, from Nevada to Manitoba, south to Kansas.

MOUNTAIN CHICKADEE — 5½"
Similar to previous, but white line over eye and black line through it. **Habitat:** Montane conifer forests; lower elevations in winter in open wood, groves, parks, towns; feeders. **Range:** S. Canada to California/ Mexican border, east through Rockies, to extreme s.w. Texas.

Plate 9. **SMALL GRAYISH BIRDS (GNATCATCHERS, TITS)**

Black-tailed
Gnatcatcher

Blue-gray
Gnatcatcher

Black-eared" form

M.

F.

Bushtit

Verdin

Plain Titmouse

Chestnut-backed
Chickadee

Bridled
Titmouse

Black-capped
Chickadee

Mountain
Chickadee

27

Plate 10. **BLUISH BIRDS**
(Jays, Kingfisher)

PINYON JAY — 10½″
All blue; *short* tail; crow-like shape. **Habitat:** Pinyon-juniper thickets, yellow pine woodlands; visits campsites, feeders. **Range:** C. Oregon, s. Montana to s.e. California, c. Arizona, New Mexico.

SCRUB JAY — 11½″
Blue head, wings, and tail; dark cheek; brownish-gray back; grayish-white below with dark throat streaks. **Habitat:** Scrub oak, pinyon-juniper woodlands; chaparral; suburbs; city-park feeders. **Range:** S. parts of Washington, Idaho, Wyoming, local to Mexican border; w. Texas. **Note:** The similar-looking, but duller, Gray-breasted Jay is a locally common inhabitant of montane oak canyons in s. Arizona, w. Texas (Chisos Mountains).

BLUE JAY — 12″
Crested; bright blue above with white wing and tail patches; whitish below with black necklace. **Habitat:** Pine-oak woodlands; parks; yards with feeders. **Range:** Mainly east of Rockies from s. Canada to c. Texas, west to e. parts of Montana, Wyoming, Colorado.

STELLER'S JAY — 13″
Crested; black head, back, and breast; deep blue wings, tail, and belly. **Habitat:** Heavy conifer forests, pine-oak woodlands; visits campsites, feeders. **Range:** S. British Columbia, Alberta, w. Montana through mountains to s. California and Mexican border, east to w. Texas.

BELTED KINGFISHER — 13½″
Gray-blue and white; bushy crest; heavy spear-like bill; gray-blue breast band; female also has chestnut band lower down. **Habitat:** Lakes, ponds, rivers, streams; marshes, swamps; bays, coasts. **Range:** S. Canada to Mexican border; winters wherever there is open water.

Plate 10. **BLUISH BIRDS**   **(JAYS, KINGFISHERS)**

crub Jay

Pinyon Jay

Blue Jay

Steller's Jay

Belted Kingfisher

29

Plate 11. BLUISH/REDDISH BIRDS

PAINTED BUNTING — 5¼ ″
Purplish-blue head; yellow-green back; bright red rump and underparts. **Habitat:** Bushes, thickets at edges of streams, swamps; plantings along roadsides; gardens, parks; yards with feeders. **Range:** S.e. portions of Kansas, New Mexico through most of Oklahoma, Texas to Mexican border; winters farther south.

LAZULI BUNTING — 5½ ″
Turquoise-blue head and rump; reddish breast and sides; white belly and wing bar; female—gray-brown above with bluish rump; buffy below; two whitish wing bars. **Habitat:** Dry open woods; brushy areas near water. **Range:** S. British Columbia, Alberta, Saskatchewan to s. California, c. Arizona, New Mexico, east to Dakotas, south to w. Oklahoma, n.w. Texas; winters north to s.e. Arizona.

VARIED BUNTING — 5 ″
Looks black in distance; close up—mixture of deep purplish-blue and brown; red nape. **Habitat:** Arid rocky slopes with thorn bush, mesquite thickets. **Range:** Along Mexican border in s. portions of Arizona, New Mexico; w. and s. Texas near Rio Grande valley; winters also in last area, and from Mexico southward.

INDIGO BUNTING — 5½ ″
All blue, but looks black in distance. **Habitat:** Woodland clearings, edges; brushy fields, rural roadsides; lawns in migration; s.w. feeders in winter. **Range:** S. Manitoba, Dakotas to s.c. Texas, southwest to s.e. Utah, Arizona, extreme s.e. California (rare); winters south of Mexican border.

BLUE GROSBEAK — 7 ″
Deep blue; chestnut wing patch and tawny wing bar; heavy bill. **Habitat:** Roadside thickets; swampy tangles; bushy fields. **Range:** C. California, Nevada, Utah, Colorado, Kansas north to s. North Dakota, south to Mexican border; winters north to s. Arizona.

MOUNTAIN BLUEBIRD — 7½ ″
Sky blue above, paler below with whitish belly. **Habitat:** Openings in conifer and mixed forests, especially in mountain meadows; winter— mainly in grasslands, deserts, agricultural areas. **Range:** S. Canada east to s.w. Manitoba, south mainly in mountains to s. California, Arizona, New Mexico, southeast to edge of Great Plains in Colorado, n.w. Oklahoma; winters from Mexico north to s.w. Washington, s. Colorado in lowlands.

WESTERN BLUEBIRD — 7 ″
Deep blue above with chestnut back patch; reddish below with white belly. **Habitat:** Wooded openings; farms, orchards, roadside trees. **Range:** S. British Columbia, Alberta, w. Montana south locally at higher elevations to Mexican border, east to New Mexico, w. Texas; winters north along Pacific Coast to Washington; inland northeast to s.w. Colorado.

Plate 11. **BLUISH/REDDISH BIRDS (FINCHES, BLUEBIRDS)**

Painted
Bunting

M.

Lazuli
Bunting

F.

Varied
Bunting

Indigo
Bunting

Blue
Grosbeak

Western
Bluebird

Mountain
Bluebird

Plate 12. GRAYISH SPARROWS

SAGE SPARROW — 5½"
Grayish above, whitish below; blackish forecrown, cheeks, and breast spot; white eye line and whisker stripe. **Habitat:** Sagebrush plains, arid scrublands; desert areas in winter. **Range:** S. Washington, Idaho, Wyoming to Mexican border; winters north to California, s. Nevada, Utah, s. New Mexico, w. Texas.

BLACK-THROATED SPARROW — 5"
Black face, throat, and breast; white stripes over and under eye; white belly. **Habitat:** Cactus and creosote-bush deserts; arid, rocky slopes. **Range:** Extreme s. parts of Oregon, Idaho, s.w. Wyoming to Mexican border, east to extreme w. Colorado, southeast to w.c. Texas; winters north to s. portions of California, Arizona, New Mexico, s.w. Texas.

BLACK-CHINNED SPARROW — 5¼"
Strikingly junco-like, with pink bill, dark eye, and gray head, rump, and below; otherwise sparrow-like, with streaked brown back and wings; black chin; female lacks black. **Habitat:** Arid, brushy slopes, canyons; chaparral, sagebrush. **Range:** C. California, s. Nevada, s.w. Utah east to New Mexico, extreme w. Texas, south to Mexican border; winters north to s.e. California, s. Arizona, New Mexico, s.w. Texas.

DARK-EYED JUNCO — 6"
Gray above, paler below; *all* forms with conspicuous pink bills, dark eyes, and white outer tail feathers. Three main types: (1) "Oregon," with black hood, brown back, and pinkish sides; (2) "Gray-headed," with pale gray head and breast, set off by bright rufous upper back; (3) "Slate-colored," with uniform slate-gray color, abruptly separated by white belly. **Habitat:** Summer—conifer and mixed forests; winter/migration—nearly all possible habitats, including city parks, suburban yards with feeders. **Range:** S. Canada to Mexican border and the Gulf.

Plate 12. **GRAYISH SPARROWS**

Black-
throated
Sparrow

Sage
Sparrow

Black-chinned
Sparrow

"Oregon"
race

"Gray-
headed"
race

"Slate-colored"
race

Dark-eyed Junco

33

Plate 13. BROWNISH SPARROWS 1

LARK SPARROW — 6″
Head handsomely patterned in chestnut, white, and black; whitish below with dark breast spot. **Habitat:** Open country with scattered trees, bushes, hedgerows, roadside fences; prairies; orchards, farms, pastures. **Range:** S. Canada to Mexican border, east to prairie states; winters north to California, s. Arizona, New Mexico, much of Texas.

WHITE-THROATED SPARROW — 6½″
White throat; yellow lores; black and white—or brown and buff—head stripes. **Habitat:** Wooded openings, clearings; lawns with shrubs in towns, city parks; feeders. **Range:** Chiefly e. North America, but winters locally in Southwest to Arizona, New Mexico, Colorado, south to Mexican border.

WHITE-CROWNED SPARROW — 7″
Black and white head stripes; pale gray face and below; *pink* bill. **Habitat:** Thickets, hedgerows adjacent to fields; roadsides; lawns with plantings; feeders. **Range:** S. British Columbia to Mexican border, east to edge of Great Plains; winters north along Pacific Coast to British Columbia, inland to s.w. Colorado.

GOLDEN-CROWNED SPARROW — 7″
Yellow crown bordered by *broad* black stripe; gray cheeks; brownish below. **Habitat:** Montane thickets, shrubs, mainly in wet areas; parks, gardens, yards; feeders. **Range:** Mainly along Pacific Coast from s. British Columbia to Mexican border.

HARRIS' SPARROW — 7½″
Black crown, face, throat, and chest; *pink* bill; grayish cheeks; white below with black spots and streaks on breast and flanks. **Habitat:** Dwarf conifer forests in high Arctic; migration/winter—open woodlands, thickets, shrubs; occasionally at feeders. **Range:** C. U.S. from e. Wyoming, South Dakota to e. Colorado, New Mexico, Texas, southeast along Mississippi River to Louisiana.

HOUSE SPARROW — 6″
Large black patch on throat and chest; gray, white, and chestnut head; female—dull, dingy brown; pale eye stripe. **Habitat:** Cities, suburbs; farms; waste areas, refuse dumps. **Range:** S. Canada to Mexican border. **Note:** Introduced from Europe.

Plate 13. **BROWNISH SPARROWS 1**

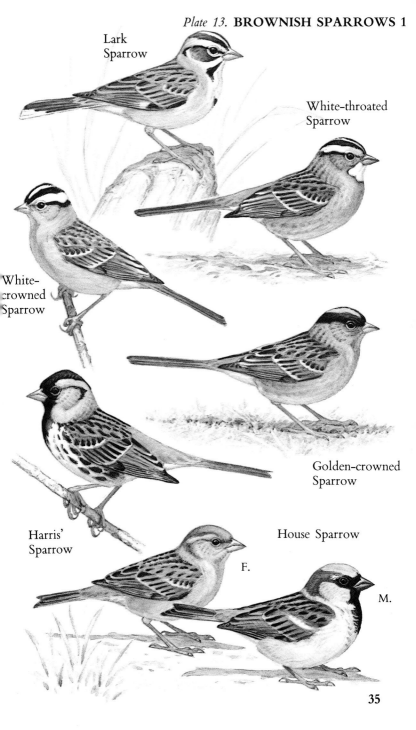

Lark
Sparrow

White-throated
Sparrow

White-
crowned
Sparrow

Golden-crowned
Sparrow

Harris'
Sparrow

House Sparrow

F.

M.

Plate 14. BROWNISH SPARROWS 2

CHIPPING SPARROW — 5¼"
Rusty cap; white and black face stripes; whitish below. **Habitat:** Wooded clearings, edges; farms, orchards, gardens; lawns with conifers. **Range:** S. Canada to Mexican border; winters north to s. parts of California, Arizona, New Mexico, Texas.

TREE SPARROW — 6¼"
Rusty cap; grayish-white below with dark breast spot; two wing bars. **Habitat:** Weedy fields, orchards, gardens, hedgerows; swampy thickets; feeders. **Range:** S. Canada to Arizona, n. California, c. Nevada, New Mexico, n. Texas.

RUFOUS-CROWNED SPARROW — 5½"
Rufous cap; gray face and breast; black whisker line. **Habitat:** Rocky slopes with grass, scattered brush. **Range:** S.w. U.S. from c. California, s. Nevada, s.w. Utah, Arizona, s.e. Colorado, New Mexico, Oklahoma to Mexican border.

SAVANNAH SPARROW — 5½"
Heavily streaked; short, notched tail; yellowish lores; white crown stripe; pink legs. **Habitat:** Grassy fields and meadows; prairies; marsh edges; sand dunes; beaches; lake and river shores. **Range:** S. Canada to Mexican border; winters north along Pacific slope to Washington, inland to Arizona, New Mexico, Oklahoma.

VESPER SPARROW — 6"
Heavily streaked; white eye ring and outer tail feathers; close up—chestnut shoulder. **Habitat:** Open country in dry grasslands; fields with scattered brush; sagebrush plains; farms, ranches. **Range:** S. Canada to Mexican border; winters north to s. parts of California, Arizona, New Mexico, c. Oklahoma.

SONG SPARROW — 6¼"
Heavily streaked; dark breast spot; long, rounded tail, often pumped in flight. **Habitat:** Bushes and thickets along edges of moist woods, ponds, streams, swamps; roadsides; gardens, lawns with shrubs; feeders. **Range:** Canada to Mexican border and Gulf; winters north to U.S./Canada border.

FOX SPARROW — 7¼"
Heavily streaked and blotched, often with dark breast spot; *reddish tail.* **Habitat:** Wooded undergrowth, dense thickets; winter—gardens, parks, yards with shrubbery; feeders. **Range:** S. British Columbia, Alberta south in mountains to s. California, c. parts of Nevada, Utah, Colorado; winters along Pacific Coast from s. British Columbia to Mexican border, inland to Arizona, New Mexico, Texas, c. Oklahoma, s. Kansas.

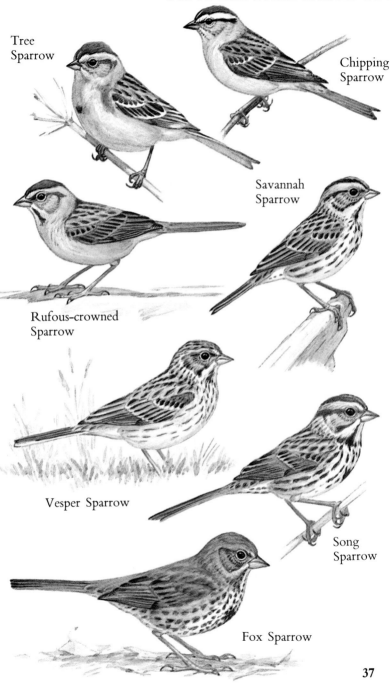

Plate 14. **BROWNISH SPARROWS 2**

Tree
Sparrow

Chipping
Sparrow

Savannah
Sparrow

Rufous-crowned
Sparrow

Vesper Sparrow

Song
Sparrow

Fox Sparrow

Plate 15. **BROWNISH BIRDS**
(Wrentit, Wrens)

WRENTIT — 6¼″
Slender with long tail, often cocked; short, thin bill; grayish-brown; pale yellowish eye. **Habitat:** Chaparral; other low, dense vegetation. **Range:** Pacific Coast from n.w. Oregon to Mexican border; in California, also local inland at low elevations in n. and c. portions.

MARSH WREN — 5″
Dark brown above, including solid, unmarked crown; whitish below; white eye line and back stripes. **Habitat:** Freshwater marshes with cattails, reeds, rushes; coastal salt and brackish marshes with giant reed *(Phragmites)*. **Range:** S. Canada to Mexican border, but local in arid Southwest; winters north along coast to Washington, inland to s. Kansas.

HOUSE WREN — 5″
Brownish above, whitish below; dark bars on wings and tail. **Habitat:** Thickets, open woodlands; orchards, gardens, parks, yards. **Range:** S. Canada to Mexican border; winters north to California, east to Texas. **Note:** Nests in cavities and bird houses.

BEWICK'S WREN — 5½″
Brownish-gray above, grayish-white below; white eye line and tail tips; often flips tail sideways. **Habitat:** Thickets, scrub, open woods; gardens, suburban yards with shrubbery; feeders. **Range:** Pacific Coast from s.w. British Columbia to California, east from Nevada to Kansas, south to Mexican border.

CANYON WREN — 5¾″
Rich reddish-brown with white throat and breast. **Habitat:** Rocky canyons, cliffs—often near water; stone buildings, dams; feeders. **Range:** S. British Columbia, Washington south through Rockies to Mexican border; s.w. South Dakota southeast to w. Oklahoma, e.c. Texas.

ROCK WREN — 6″
Grayish-brown above with rufous rump; buff below; tawny tail tips at corners. **Habitat:** Rocky areas in arid country. **Range:** S. British Columbia, Alberta, Saskatchewan to Mexican border, east to w. Dakotas, Nebraska, Kansas, Oklahoma, Texas; winters along coast north to s. British Columbia, inland to Oklahoma.

CACTUS WREN — 8″
Much larger than other wrens; chestnut crown; white eye line; streaked back; heavily barred wings and tail; conspicuous black spots below, especially on breast. **Habitat:** Deserts with cactus, mesquite, yucca, thorn scrub; also in towns in arid country with similar growth; feeders. **Range:** Mexican border north to s. California, Nevada, s.w. Utah, c. Arizona, New Mexico, c. and s.w. Texas.

Plate 15. **BROWNISH BIRDS (WRENTIT, WRENS)**

Marsh
Wren

Wrentit

House
Wren

Bewick's
Wren

Canyon
Wren

Rock
Wren

Cactus
Wren

Plate 16. BROWNISH BIRDS
(Towhees, Thrashers)

GREEN-TAILED TOWHEE — 7″
Rufous cap; olive-green back, wings, and tail; white throat with black whisker; gray face, breast, and sides; white belly. **Habitat:** Dry mountain slopes with scrub; winter—lower elevations with sage, chaparral, manzanita; feeders. **Range:** Oregon, Idaho, Montana to Mexican border; winters north to California, Arizona, New Mexico, Texas, to Gulf Coast.

RUFOUS-SIDED ("SPOTTED") TOWHEE — 8″
Black hood and upper parts; rufous sides; white belly; white back, wing, and tail spots; female—similar, but black replaced by brown. **Habitat:** Open woods; brushy fields, thickets; yards, parks; feeders. **Range:** S. Canada to Mexican border; winters on Pacific Coast, inland and north to Nevada, Utah, Colorado.

BROWN TOWHEE — 9″
Grayish-brown above, paler below; tawny or buffy throat with spotted necklace; rufous vent; interior form has rusty cap and dark spot below necklace. **Habitat:** Open country with scrub, brushy hills, canyons; parks, gardens; feeders. **Range:** Pacific Coast from s.w. Oregon to Mexican border, inland from s. Colorado, Arizona, New Mexico, s.w. Texas.

ABERT'S TOWHEE — 9″
All brown, lighter below; *black* face. **Habitat:** Desert scrub, mesquite; cottonwood-willow stands along streams in arid areas; orchards, gardens, yards; feeders. **Range:** Local in s.e. California, Nevada, s.w. Utah, w. and s. Arizona, and s.w. New Mexico to Mexican border.

SAGE THRASHER — 8½″
Grayish above; two thin white wing bars; short bill; short tail with white-tipped corners; streaked below. **Habitat:** Sagebrush; winter—deserts. **Range:** S. Canada to California, Arizona, New Mexico; winters California, Arizona, New Mexico, w. Texas south to Mexican border.

BENDIRE'S THRASHER — 10″
Grayish-brown above, paler below; mottled breast; short bill. **Habitat:** Desert scrub; grasslands; ranches. **Range:** S.e. California, s. Nevada, Utah; Arizona, w. New Mexico; winters north to s. Arizona.

CURVE-BILLED THRASHER — 11″
Similar to Bendire's Thrasher, with longer, more curved bill; breast more heavily mottled. **Habitat:** Deserts; canyons; towns, gardens. **Range:** Arizona, New Mexico, Colorado, Oklahoma, Texas.

CALIFORNIA THRASHER — 12″
Large; very long, decurved bill; gray-brown above; line over eye; dark cheek; buffy throat, gray breast; cinnamon belly and vent. **Habitat:** Chaparral along coastal foothills; inland in brush and thickets; parks, gardens, yards. **Range:** W. and c. California south to Mexican border.

Plate 16. **BROWNISH BIRDS (TOWHEES, THRASHERS)**

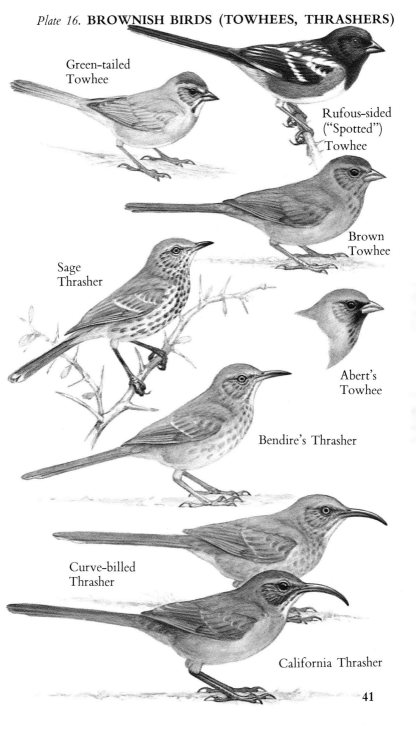

Green-tailed
Towhee

Rufous-sided
("Spotted")
Towhee

Brown
Towhee

Sage
Thrasher

Abert's
Towhee

Bendire's Thrasher

Curve-billed
Thrasher

California Thrasher

41

Plate 17. BROWNISH BIRDS
(Waxwings, Thrushes)

CEDAR WAXWING — 7″
Grayish-brown; sleek and crested; black mask and chin; yellow belly and tail tip; *white* vent. **Habitat:** Orchards, fruiting trees, vines, shrubs; open woods near water. **Range:** S. Canada to Mexican border; winters north to s. British Columbia, Montana, Dakotas.

BOHEMIAN WAXWING — 8″
Similar to Cedar Waxwing, but larger and grayer; white spots on wings; *rusty* vent. **Habitat:** Summer—conifer forests, boreal bogs; rest of year—highly nomadic, occurring wherever there are fruiting shrubs and trees, even in towns, cities. **Range:** S. Canada south through mountains to c. California, n. Arizona, New Mexico; winters throughout. **Note:** Waxwings are often very tame, and at close range the red wax-like wing spot that gives these birds their name may be seen (adults only).

VEERY — 7″
Reddish-brown above, white below with pale gray sides; breast spots indistinct. **Habitat:** Moist deciduous woods; swampy thickets; parks, yards. **Range:** S. Canada to Utah, Colorado; farther south, migrates chiefly east of plains; winters in tropics.

SWAINSON'S THRUSH — 7″
Brownish above, white below with tawny or buffy cheeks, throat, and sides; breast spots distinct; conspicuous light eye ring. **Habitat:** Moist woodlands, swampy thickets; parks, yards. **Range:** S. Canada to c. California, n. Arizona, New Mexico; winters in tropics.

HERMIT THRUSH — 7″
Olive-brown above with distinct rufous tail; white below; distinct breast spots; conspicuous light eye ring. **Habitat:** Mixed woods, thickets; parks, yards. **Range:** S. Canada to Mexican border; winters along coast north to Washington, inland to Nevada, s. Utah, c. New Mexico, s. Oklahoma, nearly throughout Texas. **Note:** Often raises tail slowly.

VARIED THRUSH — 9½″
Blue-gray above, orange below; orange eye stripe, wing bars, and patches; black mask and broad breast band. **Habitat:** Thick, wet conifer forests; winter—also hardwoods, thickets, brushy ravines; feeders in severe winters. **Range:** Chiefly Pacific Northwest from s. British Columbia, Alberta through mountains to Idaho, n.w. Montana, n. California; winters south to California/Mexican border.

AMERICAN ROBIN — 10″
Rusty breast; brownish-gray back; blackish head and tail; yellow bill. **Habitat:** Lawns, golf courses, towns, parks, farms, wooded clearings. **Range:** S. Canada to Mexican border; winters throughout, except in mountains and northern Plains States.

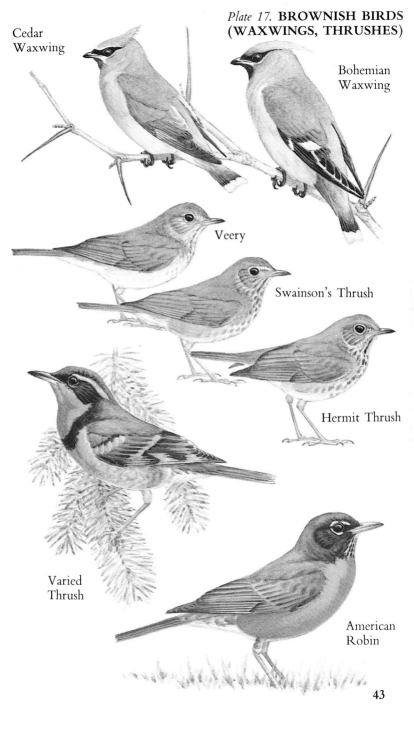

Cedar
Waxwing

Plate 17. **BROWNISH BIRDS
(WAXWINGS, THRUSHES)**

Bohemian
Waxwing

Veery

Swainson's Thrush

Hermit Thrush

Varied
Thrush

American
Robin

43

Plate 18. GRASSLAND BIRDS

CHESTNUT-COLLARED LONGSPUR — 6″

Black crown, breast, and belly; chestnut nape; buff and white cheeks and throat; black crescent-shaped ear patch. **Habitat:** Tall-grass plains, prairies. **Range:** S. parts of Alberta, Saskatchewan, Manitoba through Montana, Dakotas, e. Wyoming, w. Nebraska, n. Colorado, east to w. Minnesota; winters mainly from Arizona, New Mexico, Oklahoma, Texas to Mexican border.

LAPLAND LONGSPUR — 6½″

Similar to preceding, but black head and breast; also white vertical stripe on neck and in front of wing (not shown); winter—breast much duller; mostly lacks black and chestnut areas; streaky. **Habitat:** Prairies, fields, airports. **Range:** Breeds in high Arctic; winters from s. Canada to s. California, east through Great Plains, south to n. Texas. **Note:** Only the winter plumage is illustrated here; breeding dress attained in high Arctic.

SNOW BUNTING — 7″

Chiefly white with black and brown patches; in flight—large white wing patches. **Habitat:** Ground bird of plains, prairies; airports, golf courses; grass flats, shores. **Range:** Breeds in high Arctic; winters from s. Canada to e. Oregon, Idaho, n. parts of Utah, Colorado, Nebraska.

WATER PIPIT — 6½″

Grayish-brown above; buffy breast with dark streaks; white outer tail feathers; slender bill; wags tail. **Habitat:** Ground bird of plains, prairies; freshly plowed and burned-over fields; airports, golf courses; lake and river shores; beaches, mud flats. **Range:** Breeds from s. British Columbia, Alberta, south in higher mountains to n. Arizona, New Mexico; winters from Washington to Mexican border, inland in Nevada and Plains States from Kansas to Texas and Gulf Coast.

HORNED LARK — 7½″

Black head and chest patches; white facial pattern; yellowish throat; brown above, whitish below. **Habitat:** Ground bird of plains, prairies; short-grass fields; airports, golf courses; lake and river shores; coastal flats, beaches. **Range:** S. Canada to Mexican border.

DICKCISSEL — 6¼″

Black patch on yellow breast; chestnut wing patch; gray head; two white face stripes; female—white throat; yellow breast patch. **Habitat:** Grass-lands, meadows, hayfields, especially those with alfalfa and clover; prairies; occasionally at feeders. **Range:** C. plains and prairies from Saskatchewan, Manitoba to Texas and Gulf; winters in tropics.

WESTERN MEADOWLARK — 9½″

Broad black **V** on bright yellow breast; mottled brown above; white outer tail feathers, conspicuous in flight. **Habitat:** Grassy fields; airports, golf courses. **Range:** S. Canada to Mexican border; winters north along coast to s.w. British Columbia, inland to Idaho, Wyoming, Nebraska.

Plate 18. **GRASSLAND BIRDS**

Chestnut-collared
Longspur

summer

Lapland
Longspur

winter

winter

Snow
Bunting

winter

Water Pipit

Horned
Lark

Western
Meadowlark

Dickcissel

Plate 19. BLACKISH BIRDS 1

PHAINOPEPLA — 7½″
Glossy black; crested; broad white wing patch, conspicuous in flight; long tail; red eye at close range. **Habitat:** Arid country with mesquite, mistletoe, paloverde, other scrub; scattered oak, pepper trees. **Range:** California, s. Nevada, Utah, Arizona, New Mexico, w. Texas to Mexican border; winters in desert areas north to s. California, Arizona, s.w. New Mexico.

LARK BUNTING — 7″
Black with conspicuous white wing patch; fall/winter male, female—streaked, sparrow-like, with wing patch. **Habitat:** Plains, prairies with mixture of grass, scrub, sagebrush; dry areas in winter—chiefly deserts. **Range:** S. Alberta east to s.w. Manitoba, south through Montana and Dakotas to Mexican border; winters north to s. Arizona, New Mexico, most of n. and c. Texas to extreme s. and w. Oklahoma.

BOBOLINK — 7″
Mainly black; white wing patch, lower back, and rump; tawny-buff nape; fall male, female—buff below, dark brown streaks above. **Habitat:** Grassy fields, meadows; mainly marshes in fall. **Range:** S. Canada to Oregon, Colorado, Nebraska, then southeast in fall; winters in s. South America.

STARLING — 8″
Black at distance; chunky, short-tailed; spring/summer—iridescent green and purple; *yellow* bill; fall/winter—similar, but with white spots; *dark* bill. **Habitat:** From large cities to beaches, wooded clearings; also lawns, fields, marshes, shores, refuse dumps. **Range:** Throughout from s. Canada to Mexican border. **Note:** Introduced from Europe.

BROWN-HEADED COWBIRD — 7″
Glossy black with brown head; stubby finch-like bill; female—all gray (not shown). **Habitat:** Farms, fields, lawns, roadsides; wooded edges, clearings; villages, city parks; feeders. **Range:** S. Canada to Mexican border; winters north to California, Nevada, Arizona, New Mexico, Texas, Kansas. **Note:** See remarks under Bronzed Cowbird (p. 48).

RED-WINGED BLACKBIRD — M 9″; F 7″
Black with bright red shoulders, edged yellowish; female—smaller, brownish, with heavy, dark streaks; light eye stripe. **Habitat:** Marshes, meadows, hayfields; lightly wooded swamps; parks; suburban feeders. **Range:** S. Canada to Mexican border; winters north to U.S./Canada border.

YELLOW-HEADED BLACKBIRD — 9½″
Black with bright golden-yellow head and breast; white wing patch. **Habitat:** Freshwater marshes; ponds, streams with reedy borders; ranches, farms, fields. **Range:** S. Canada to Mexican border; winters north to c. California, s. Arizona, New Mexico, w. Texas.

Plate 19. **BLACKISH BIRDS 1**

Phainopepla

Lark
Bunting

Bobolink

winter

Starling

summer

Brown-headed
Cowbird

Yellow-headed
Blackbird

M.

Red-winged
Blackbird

F.

47

Plate 20. **BLACKISH BIRDS 2**

BREWER'S BLACKBIRD — 9″

Black at distance; close up—iridescent purple head, greenish body; *yellow* eye; female—grayish; *dark* eye. **Habitat:** Open country—farms, fields, lake and river shores; city parks, suburban lawns; feeders. **Range:** S. Canada to Mexican border; winters north to s. British Columbia, Idaho, Wyoming, Dakotas, s.w. Nebraska.

BRONZED (RED-EYED) COWBIRD — 8″

Black at distance; close up—bronzy with blue-black wings and tail; *red* eye. **Habitat:** Open country with scattered trees, scrub; irrigated ranches, farmland; suburban lawns. **Range:** C. and s. Arizona, s.w. New Mexico, mainly s.c. Texas to Mexican border and the Gulf. **Note:** Unlike other birds, both cowbird females are parasitic, laying their eggs in other birds' nests!

COMMON GRACKLE — 12″

Black at distance; close up—iridescent blue, purple, and green; *yellow* eye; long keel- or wedge-shaped tail. **Habitat:** Farms, fields; marshes, roadsides with conifers; lawns, parks; feeders. **Range:** West to s. Alberta, Montana, Wyoming, Colorado, New Mexico; winters north to s.e. Nebraska, west to c. Texas.

GREAT-TAILED GRACKLE — M 18″, F 15″

Black at distance; crow-sized, but slender, long, wedge-shaped tail; close up—iridescent purple and blue; *yellow* eye; female—smaller; dark brown above, cinnamon below, darker on belly; tawny-buff eyebrow; *yellow* eye. **Habitat:** Open areas, wetlands, ranches, towns, parks. **Range:** S.w. Louisiana to s.e. California, along Gulf and Mexican border, north to s. Colorado, c. Kansas.

BLACK-BILLED MAGPIE — 20″

Generally black at distance, iridescent green and blue close up; white belly; very long, wedge-shaped tail; two large white wing patches, very conspicuous in flight. **Habitat:** Ranches; sagebrush plains; thickets; scattered trees along water courses; at northern edge of range—also towns; feeders in severe winters. **Range:** S. Canada to s.c. California (*not* along Pacific Coast), New Mexico, east to edge of Great Plains as far as e. Kansas.

AMERICAN CROW — 19″

All black; large and chunky; short-tailed; tail *fan-shaped* in flight. **Habitat:** Farms, fields, woods, shores, parks, towns; suburban feeders. **Range:** S. Canada to California/Mexican border, c. Arizona, s. New Mexico, mainly c. and e. Texas; winters north to U.S./Canada border.

NORTHERN RAVEN — 24″

All black; larger than American Crow; short-tailed; tail *wedge-shaped* in flight. **Habitat:** Boreal, coniferous forests; mountains, even above tree line; rocky canyons, deserts; coastal cliffs; visits campsites, refuse dumps, where it scavenges. **Range:** S. British Columbia, Alberta south through Rockies to Mexican border; east to foothills of mountains; local in s.w. Texas.

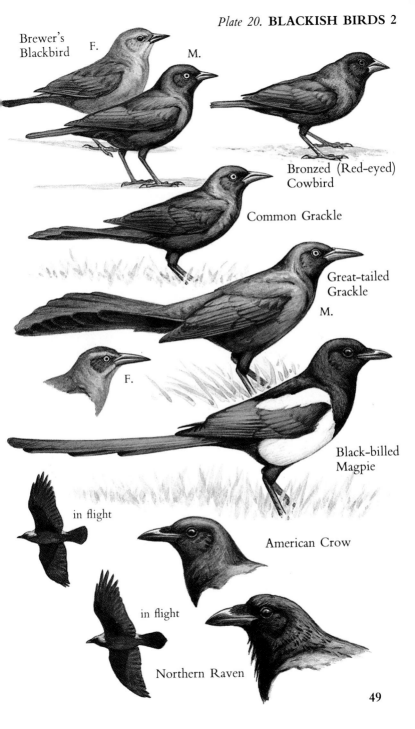

Plate 20. **BLACKISH BIRDS 2**

Brewer's Blackbird F. M.

Bronzed (Red-eyed) Cowbird

Common Grackle

Great-tailed Grackle

M.

F.

Black-billed Magpie

in flight

American Crow

in flight

Northern Raven

49

Plate 21. **TREE CLINGERS**

PYGMY NUTHATCH — 4″

Blue-gray above, buff below; grayish-brown cap; whitish nape at close range. **Habitat:** Montane pine forests. **Range:** S. British Columbia, local from Washington, Idaho, Montana south through mountains to Mexican border; very local in e. Montana, Wyoming, Nevada, w. Texas.

RED-BREASTED NUTHATCH — 4½″

Black and white striped face; blue-gray above, *rusty* below; male—*black* cap; female—*gray* cap. **Habitat:** Summer—conifer forests; winter—chiefly pines; migration—also hardwoods; feeders. **Range:** S. Canada to Mexican border; winters chiefly in lowlands.

WHITE-BREASTED NUTHATCH — 5½″

Blue-gray above, *white* below; male—*black* cap; female—*gray* cap. **Habitat:** Deciduous forests; swampy woodlands; shade trees; feeders. **Range:** S. Canada to Mexican border; local in Southwest. **Note:** Nuthatches are our only birds which descend with head down.

BROWN CREEPER — 5″

Brown above, white below; slender, decurved bill; stiff, pointed tail. **Habitat:** Woodlands; shade trees; shrubs, thickets. **Range:** S. Canada to Mexican border; local in Southwest.

DOWNY WOODPECKER — 6½″

Black and white pattern; white back and below; red hindcrown; *short* bill; female—similar, but *no* red. **Habitat:** Open woodlands; orchards; shade trees; shrubbery; feeders. **Range:** S. Canada to Mexican border; local in Southwest.

HAIRY WOODPECKER — 9½″

Very similar to Downy Woodpecker, but larger and with *long* bill. **Habitat:** Forests; shade trees; feeders. **Range:** S. Canada to Mexican border; local in Southwest.

LADDER-BACKED WOODPECKER — 7″

White face with *black* markings; red crown *extensive*. **Habitat:** Deserts; canyons; arid scrub near water. **Range:** S.w. California, s. Nevada, s.w. Utah, Arizona, New Mexico, s.e. Colorado, w. Oklahoma to most of w. and c. Texas.

NUTTALL'S WOODPECKER — 7″

Similar to Ladder-backed Woodpecker, but *black* face with *white* markings; red restricted to *hindcrown*. **Habitat:** Wooded slopes, canyons; chaparral; river groves; orchards. **Range:** Mainly w. and c. California from extreme north to Mexican border (Baja California).

Plate 21. **TREE CLINGERS**

Pygmy
Nuthatch

Brown
Creeper

Red-breasted
Nuthatch

White-breasted
Nuthatch

Downy
Woodpecker

Ladder-backed
Woodpecker

Nuttall's
Woodpecker

Hairy
Woodpecker

51

Plate 22. **WOODPECKERS 1**

YELLOW-BELLIED SAPSUCKER — 9″

Long white wing patch; red, black, and white head; yellowish belly; female—similar, but white throat. **Habitat:** Light open woodlands; orchards; shade trees. **Range:** S. Canada to Mexican border; rare to absent in Pacific and Great Plains states; winters mainly in southern parts.

RED-BREASTED SAPSUCKER — 9″

Similar to Yellow-bellied, but entire head and breast red. **Habitat:** Coniferous, mixed forests in mountains. **Range:** Chiefly Pacific slope from s. British Columbia to Mexican border, but nearly throughout California.

WILLIAMSON'S SAPSUCKER — 9½″

Male—mostly black with long white wing patch and narrow head stripes; small red throat patch; yellow belly. Female very different—brown head; dark brown and white bars on back, wings, and sides. **Habitat:** Dry montane conifer forests. **Range:** Extreme s. British Columbia to Mexican border; east to w. Montana, c. Wyoming, Colorado, w. New Mexico; winters north to Oregon, Nevada, Utah, Arizona, New Mexico.

GOLDEN-FRONTED WOODPECKER — 9½″

Similar to Gila Woodpecker, but male with yellow above bill and with orange nape. **Habitat:** Arid country with mesquite; dry open woodlands; pecan orchards; river groves. **Range:** S.w. Oklahoma, most of w. Texas to Gulf and Mexican border.

GILA WOODPECKER — 9″

Zebra-backed; grayish below; male—small red cap. **Habitat:** Deserts, especially with saguaro cactus; river groves in arid country; towns. **Range:** S.e. California, c. Arizona, s.w. New Mexico.

NORTHERN FLICKER — 13″

Brown back with black bars; spotted below; white rump; red facial stripe on gray cheek (male only); red wing lining (yellow in s.w. deserts). **Habitat:** Open woodlands; shade trees; parks, suburban lawns; deserts in Southwest; often feeds on ground. **Range:** S. Canada to Mexican border; winters nearly throughout.

Plate 22. **WOODPECKERS 1**

Williamson's
Sapsucker

M.

F.

Yellow-bellied
Sapsucker

Red-
breasted
Sapsucker

Golden-
fronted
Woodpecker

Northern
Flicker

Gila
Woodpecker

53

Plate 23. **WOODPECKERS 2**

ACORN WOODPECKER — 9″

Black and white face; red crown; black back, tail, and wings; white rump. **Habitat:** Chiefly oak-pine forests; visits campsites, hummingbird feeders. **Range:** S.w. Oregon, California to Mexican border, Arizona, New Mexico, extreme w. Texas.

LEWIS' WOODPECKER — 11″

Mainly black above, including wings, rump, and tail; gray collar and breast; rose-pink belly; dark red face. **Habitat:** Open forests in clearings, burns. **Range:** S. British Columbia, Alberta to Mexican border, east to edge of Great Plains in Wyoming, Colorado, New Mexico; winters north to Oregon, Nevada, Utah, s.w. Colorado.

RED-HEADED WOODPECKER — 9½″

Red head; large white wing patches, rump, and underparts; black back, tail, and wings. **Habitat:** Groves, orchards, shade trees; farms; wooded swamps; river bottoms. **Range:** Mainly east of Rockies from s. Canada, Montana to s.c. New Mexico.

WHITE-HEADED WOODPECKER — 9″

Mostly black with white forehead, cheeks, and throat; white wing patches, evident in flight; male—red nape. **Habitat:** Montane conifer forests. **Range:** Washington, Oregon, w. Idaho, w. Nevada, most of California to Mexican border.

THREE-TOED WOODPECKER — 9″

Black and white with bars on back and sides; male—*yellow* crown. **Habitat:** Montane conifer forests. **Range:** S. Canada (not Saskatchewan) south in Rockies to c. parts of Arizona, New Mexico.

PILEATED WOODPECKER — 18″

Very large—crow-sized; red crest; black and white face and neck; black body; white wing linings, conspicuous in overhead flight. **Habitat:** Mainly mixed forests, but also open woods and parks, even visiting feeders. **Range:** S. Canada, but local in west; south to c. California, in Rockies to s.c. Idaho, w. Montana; also to e. Dakotas, southeast to Kansas, Oklahoma, c. Texas.

Acorn Woodpecker

Plate 23. **WOODPECKERS 2**

Lewis' Woodpecker

Red-headed Woodpecker

White-headed Woodpecker

Pileated Woodpecker

Three-toed Woodpecker

55

Plate 24. SWALLOWS

BARN SWALLOW — 7″
Deeply forked tail; deep blue above; chestnut throat; cinnamon breast and belly. **Habitat:** Farms, fields, marshes, ponds; nests inside barns and under bridges. **Range:** S. Canada to Mexican border; winters in tropics.

CLIFF SWALLOW — 6″
Square tail; buff rump; whitish forehead; chestnut to blackish throat; grayish-white breast and belly. **Habitat:** Farms, marshes, lakes, rivers, cliffs; nests on cliffs and stone buildings. **Range:** S. Canada to Mexican border; winters in tropics.

VIOLET-GREEN SWALLOW — 5½″
Glossy green and purple above; white on face, sides of rump, and below. **Habitat:** Canyons, cliffs; open mixed forests, clearings at high altitudes; nests in hollow trees and rock crevices; migration/winter—low elevations in fields, meadows; around towns. **Range:** S. British Columbia, Alberta to Mexican border, east through Rockies to New Mexico, extreme w. Texas; winters north to Pacific Coast of c. California, locally to s. Arizona.

TREE SWALLOW — 6″
Glossy blue-green above, white below. **Habitat:** Open country near water; marshes, meadows; wooded swamps, especially those with dead trees; nests in holes in dead trees and bird boxes. **Range:** S. Canada to s. California, Nevada, c. Arizona, New Mexico, local east of Rockies to Nebraska, Kansas; migrates through Oklahoma, Texas; winters from Mexican border north to c. California, s.w. Arizona, s. Texas.

BANK SWALLOW — 5″
Dark brown above; white below with brown chest band. **Habitat:** Open country; over land, and water—nests in holes in sand and gravel banks. **Range:** Breeds locally from s. Canada to n. and c. portions of Mexican border states (*not* Arizona or Texas), but migrates through all states; winters in tropics.

ROUGH-WINGED SWALLOW — 5½″
Light brown above, whitish below with dull grayish-brown throat and chest. **Habitat:** Near water—nests in banks and culverts, also under bridges. **Range:** S. Canada to Mexican border; winters chiefly south of border, locally north to s. parts of California, Arizona, Texas.

PURPLE MARTIN — 8″
Glossy purplish-blue; female—similar but duller above; gray throat and breast—whitish belly. **Habitat:** Open country near water—nests around farms and towns in bird houses, also in tree holes. **Range:** Breeds locally from s. Canada to Mexican border, but rare or absent over much of West; migrates throughout; winters in tropics.

Plate 24. **SWALLOWS**

Barn
Swallow

Cliff Swallow

Violet-green
Swallow

Bank
Swallow

Rough-winged
Swallow

Tree
Swallow

M.

F.

Purple
Martin

57

Plate 25. SWIFTS, NIGHTJARS

VAUX'S SWIFT — 4½″
Black at distance; pale whitish throat at close range; long, curved, pointed wings. **Habitat:** Open woodlands near water—nests in hollow trees; migration—open sky. **Range:** S. British Columbia, Washington, Idaho, w. Montana, local south along Pacific Coast to c. California; local migrant in s. Arizona; winters south of Mexican border.

WHITE-THROATED SWIFT — 6½″
Body black and white from below; *notched* tail—black; long, curved, pointed wings. **Habitat:** Mountains, cliffs, canyons; nests in cliff crevices; migration—open sky. **Range:** S. British Columbia south through mountains to Mexican border, east to edge of Great Plains; winters north to c. California, s. Arizona, New Mexico, w. Texas.

BLACK SWIFT — 7½″
All black; *notched* tail; long, curved, pointed wings. **Habitat:** Mountains, cliffs—often nests behind waterfalls; migration—open sky. **Range:** Local from s. British Columbia, s.w. Alberta south through Pacific States to s. California; also n.w. Montana, c. Utah, w. Colorado; local migrant in Arizona, New Mexico; winters in tropics.

COMMON NIGHTHAWK — 9½″
Long, pointed wings; in flight, prominent white wing band. **Habitat:** Open country; over towns, cities; open pineland; wooded clearings; farms, fields, pastures, plains. **Range:** S. Canada to Mexican border and Gulf; winters in tropics.

POORWILL — 7½″
Rounded wings; generally mottled grayish-brown; when flushed from ground, looks like a large moth; at close range—broad white chest band. **Habitat:** Arid open country with rocks, scattered brush. **Range:** Extreme s. Canada to Mexican border; local migrant east to edge of Great Plains, winters north to s. California, Arizona, s.w. New Mexico, s.c. Texas.

Plate 25. **SWIFTS, NIGHTJARS**

Vaux's Swift

White-throated Swift

Black Swift

in flight

Poorwill

on ground

Common Nighthawk

59

Plate 26. HUMMINGBIRDS

CALLIOPE — 3″
Our smallest bird; unique among hummers in having a "split" gorget, i.e., purplish-red rays or streaks on white throat, the streaks extending to sides of neck; glittering golden-green above; greenish flanks; white breast and belly. **Habitat:** Summer—high mountain forest openings, canyons, meadows; migration—lowland areas with scrub, thickets, desert. **Range:** S. Canada to California, Nevada, Utah, Colorado; migrates through Southwest to Arizona, w. New Mexico; winters south of border.

RUFOUS — 3½″
Bright reddish-brown above and on sides; fiery, orange-red gorget; white chest and side of neck. **Habitat:** Forest edges, clearings; mountain meadows; lowland streams; parks, gardens. **Range:** S. Canada, n.w. California, c. Idaho, w. Montana; migrates east to edge of Rockies; winters chiefly in Mexico, rarely north to s. California, Arizona, Texas.

ALLEN'S — 3½″
Very similar to Rufous, but crown and back iridescent green. **Habitat:** Similar to that of Rufous. **Range:** Pacific Coast from s.w. Oregon to s. California; winters in n.w. Mexico, Channel Islands, rarely s. Arizona.

ANNA'S — 4″
Rose-red cap and gorget, the latter extending slightly down sides. **Habitat:** Open woodlands; chaparral, scrub; parks, gardens. **Range:** Mainly Pacific Coast from s. British Columbia to Mexican border; also c. and s. Arizona.

BROAD-TAILED — 4″
Gleaming rose-red gorget. **Habitat:** Montane meadows with thickets; openings in mixed woodlands. **Range:** From e. Idaho, w. Montana, Wyoming to Mexican border, west to e. California, east to w. Texas; winters south of border.

COSTA'S — 3¼″
Deep purple cap; purple gorget extending way down sides. **Habitat:** Deserts, chaparral, scrub; parks, gardens. **Range:** California, Nevada, Arizona, New Mexico to border; winters north to s. California, Arizona.

BLACK-CHINNED — 3½″
Gorget with black chin and bluish-purple throat, snow-white chest; greenish sides; at distance—gorget looks black; female—greenish above, whitish below. **Habitat:** Deserts, scrub, chaparral, canyons, river groves; parks, gardens. **Range:** S. Canada to Mexican border, east to Idaho, Montana, Wyoming, Colorado, Texas; winters south of border.

BROAD-BILLED — 3¾″
Black in distance; close up—all dark green with white vent; *red* bill with black tip; in good light—dark *blue* gorget. **Habitat:** Desert canyons; slopes with agaves, cacti, mesquite, ocotillo; woodland openings. **Range:** S.e. Arizona, s.w. New Mexico, w. Texas; winters in Mexico.

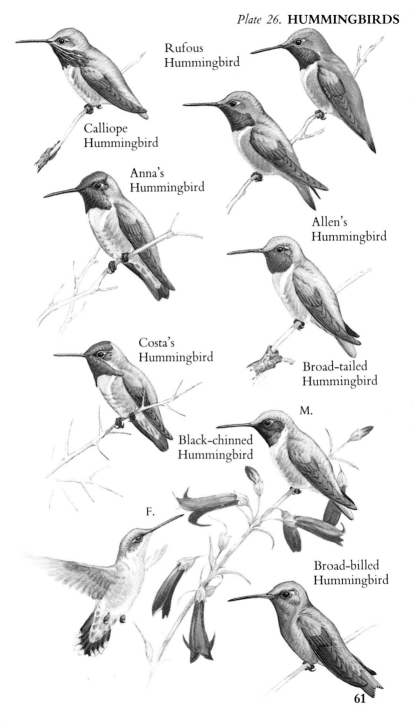

Plate 26. **HUMMINGBIRDS**

Rufous
Hummingbird

Calliope
Hummingbird

Anna's
Hummingbird

Allen's
Hummingbird

Costa's
Hummingbird

Broad-tailed
Hummingbird

M.

Black-chinned
Hummingbird

F.

Broad-billed
Hummingbird

61

Plate 27. CUCKOO, PIGEONS

YELLOW-BILLED CUCKOO — 12″
Brown above, white below; slender; long-tailed; bill slightly downcurved, lower half yellow; large white patches on underside of tail; rufous flash in wings, evident in flight. **Habitat:** Open woodlands; thickets; overgrown fields; orchards. **Range:** South Dakota, s. Wyoming, Utah, c. Nevada, s. California to Mexican border; winters in tropics.

MOURNING DOVE — 12″
Slender; fawn-colored; long, pointed tail, edged white. **Habitat:** Open country; lawns, parks; feeders. **Range:** S. Canada to Mexican border; winters nearly throughout, except Canada and northern border states.

WHITE-WINGED DOVE — 12″
Generally gray; large white wing patches, most conspicuous in flight; rounded tail, corners tipped white. **Habitat:** Arid country with mesquite, paloverde, saguaro cactus; riverine woodlands, orchards; feeders. **Range:** S.e. California, s. Arizona, s.w. New Mexico, southeast along Mexican border to southernmost Texas on the Rio Grande.

GROUND DOVE — 6½″
Very small; pinkish-gray; *short, rounded,* dark tail; rufous outer wing patch, conspicuous in flight; at close range—scaly head and breast. **Habitat:** Open sandy areas with scattered trees, scrub; orchards, gardens; ranches; towns; feeders. **Range:** S. California, Arizona, New Mexico, Texas.

INCA DOVE — 8″
Similar to Ground Dove, but with *long, pointed,* white-edged tail. **Habitat:** Arid areas with cactus, mesquite; gardens, parks, yards; feeders. **Range:** S.e. California, s. Arizona, New Mexico, much of c. and s. Texas.

SPOTTED DOVE — 13″
Easily identified by black collar with white spots; long, rounded tail with white edge. **Habitat:** Suburban gardens, yards, city parks; farms; wooded edges. **Range:** S. California. **Note:** Introduced from China.

BAND-TAILED PIGEON — 15″
Large and plump; gray; fan-shaped tail with dark band across middle; purplish head and breast; at close range—narrow white crescent on nape; yellow bill with black tip. **Habitat:** Montane oak, pine forests; winter— also parks, suburban gardens; feeders. **Range:** Mountains along Pacific Coast from s. British Columbia to Mexican border; inland mountains from Nevada, Utah, Colorado to s. Arizona, New Mexico, w. Texas; winters chiefly south of border, locally in California.

ROCK (DOMESTIC) PIGEON — 13″
Plump; blue-gray body; short, fan-shaped tail; white rump; two black wing bars; iridescent neck patch. **Habitat:** Rock cliffs—its ancestral home; buildings in cities, towns; parks, farms; dumps. **Range:** Throughout, from Canada to Mexican border. **Note:** Introduced from Europe. Many color varieties occur, ranging from black to white.

Plate 27. **CUCKOO, PIGEONS**

Yellow-billed Cuckoo

Ground Dove

Mourning Dove

Inca Dove

White-winged Dove

Spotted Dove

Band-tailed Pigeon

Rock (Domestic) Pigeon

63

Plate 28. SMALL GAMEBIRDS

BOBWHITE — 9½″
Small chicken-like bird; black and white face; female—similar, but with tawny-buff face. **Habitat:** Farmland; hedgerows, roadsides; fields with thickets, dense brush; feeders. **Range:** West to e. portions of Wyoming, Colorado, New Mexico, south through most of Texas.

SCALED QUAIL — 11″
Grayish-brown with white-tipped crest; scaled over much of body. **Habitat:** Arid areas with thorn scrub; dry grasslands. **Range:** Local from s.e. Colorado, s.w. Kansas through w. Oklahoma, Texas, New Mexico, s.e. Arizona.

MOUNTAIN QUAIL — 11″
Brown above; gray crown and breast; *chestnut* throat and sides; black and white streaks on neck and flanks; conspicuous long, *upright* head plume(s). **Habitat:** Mountain slopes, both forested and open, but almost always with undergrowth. **Range:** Local from Canadian border south through Washington, w. Idaho, Oregon, Utah, w. Nevada, California to Mexican border.

GAMBEL'S QUAIL — 11″
Variegated—brown, gray, buff, and chestnut; *black* throat and *belly patch;* conspicuous black head plume—curved forward. **Habitat:** Desert scrub; thickets; common at *feeders.* **Range:** Mexican border north to s.e. California, s. Nevada, Arizona, New Mexico, w. Texas; local north to Utah, Colorado.

CALIFORNIA QUAIL — 11″
Similar to Gambel's Quail, but with *chestnut belly patch* and more scaling. **Habitat:** *Woodland* edges; clearings; coastal scrub (chaparral); farms; parks; suburban yards—often near water. **Range:** Chiefly Pacific slope from s. British Columbia to Mexican border; inland east to Idaho, Nevada, Utah, where apparently introduced. **Note:** The habitat differences in these species help to distinguish them.

CHUKAR PARTRIDGE — 13″
Grayish-brown body with buff belly and vent; *red* bill and legs; prominent *black line* outlining white throat; black side stripes. **Habitat:** Arid, rocky slopes; canyons. **Range:** Local throughout much of West in mountainous areas. **Note:** Introduced from Eurasia.

GRAY PARTRIDGE — 13″
Prominent *rusty face* and *throat;* chestnut side stripes and belly patch; otherwise brown above, gray below. **Habitat:** Open agricultural districts; grassy plains, prairies. **Range:** S. Canada, n. U.S. to c. states. **Note:** Introduced from Eurasia.

64

Plate 28. **SMALL GAMEBIRDS**

Bobwhite

Scaled
Quail

Mountain
Quail

Gambel's
Quail

Chukar
Partridge

California
Quail

Gray
Partridge

65

Plate 29. **ROADRUNNER, LARGE GAMEBIRDS**

ROADRUNNER — 22″

Large *long-tailed* ground cuckoo with *bushy crest;* heavily streaked. **Habitat:** Stony deserts with scrub, mesquite; sometimes bold and confiding, frequenting feeders, patios, even house rooftops! **Range:** S.w. U.S. from c. California east to extreme w. parts of Arkansas, Louisiana; also s.w. Missouri. **Note:** Most numerous in s.w. deserts.

WILD TURKEY — M 48″; F 36″

Huge gallinaceous bird; bare head and neck with blue and red wattles; male—bristly "beard" on breast; female—smaller and duller without much ornamentation. **Habitat:** Hardwood forests, mainly at higher elevations. **Range:** Chiefly Rocky Mountains, but local over much of West. **Note:** Wild Turkeys have chestnut tail tips, domesticated varieties white ones.

RING-NECKED PHEASANT — M 33″; F 23″

Very long, pointed tail; white neck ring; iridescent purple and green head; scarlet face wattles; female—smaller and much duller; mottled brown above, tawny-buff below. **Habitat:** Farmland with hedgerows, cornfields; thickets near marshes, swamps; feeders. **Range:** Nearly throughout, but local over much of Southwest. **Note:** Introduced from w. Asia.

SHARP-TAILED GROUSE — 17″

Brownish; covered with *speckles and spots* (*not* barred as in Prairie Chickens). **Habitat:** Grasslands; savannas; sagebrush; wooded edges. **Range:** Local from s. Canada to c. U.S.; *not* along Pacific slope.

SAGE GROUSE — 28″

Large; brownish-gray above; black throat, neck, and belly; white breast; long, pointed, spiked tail; at close range—male has yellow eye wattles. **Habitat:** Open sagebrush plains. **Range:** S. Alberta, Saskatchewan south through the plains, foothills of Rocky Mountain States, west to e. Washington, Oregon, California, south to n.e. New Mexico.

BLUE GROUSE — 18″

Deep gray body; whitish rump; black tail; pale gray band at tail tip; orange head wattle or "comb" above eye. **Habitat:** Conifer (fir) forests, mainly at high altitudes. **Range:** S. British Columbia, Alberta, in mountains south to c. California, n. Arizona, s.w. New Mexico.

RUFFED GROUSE — 17″

Variously brown to gray above, paler below; black neck patch; broad black band near tail tip; slight crest. **Habitat:** Open mixed woodlands; forest clearings. **Range:** S. Canada to n. California, Utah, extreme s.w. South Dakota (Black Hills).

Plate 29. **ROADRUNNER, LARGE GAMEBIRDS**

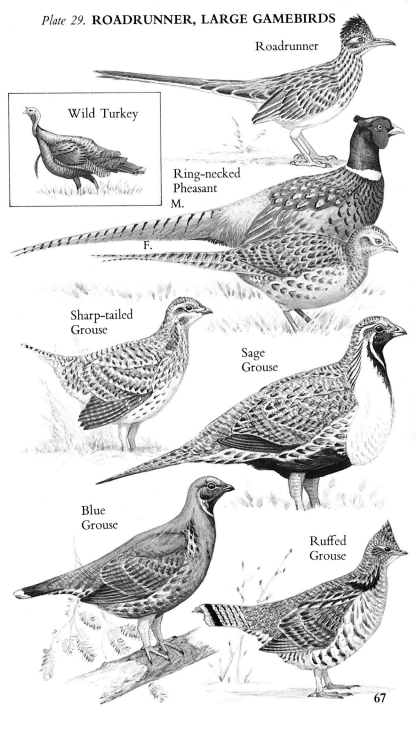

Roadrunner

Wild Turkey

Ring-necked
Pheasant
M.

F.

Sharp-tailed
Grouse

Sage
Grouse

Blue
Grouse

Ruffed
Grouse

Plate 30. HAWKS 1
(Vultures, Eagles)

BLACK VULTURE — 25″

Large white patches near wing tips, evident in flight; short tail; distinctive flight—several flaps and a glide; at close range—small gray head (see also under Turkey Vulture). **Habitat:** Similar to that of Turkey Vulture, but limited mainly to low elevations. **Range:** Mexican border and Gulf to s. Arizona, Texas, e. Oklahoma.

TURKEY VULTURE — 28″

In flight, wings held in shallow V, tilting from side to side; undersurface of wings two-toned; at close range—small red head; immature—gray head (see also head color under Black Vulture). **Habitat:** Generally open country—wherever carrion is found, both in mountains and lowlands. **Range:** S. Canada to Mexican border; winters north to California, Arizona, New Mexico, s. Kansas.

GOLDEN EAGLE — 33″

All brown; at close range—golden wash on head and neck. **Habitat:** Mountains, plains, canyons, deserts. **Range:** S. Canada to Mexican border, rare in c. and s. Texas. **Note:** Immatures have much black and white in tail.

BALD EAGLE — 33″

White head and tail; dark brown body and wings; large yellow bill. **Habitat:** Lakes, rivers, seacoasts. **Range:** S. Canada to Mexican border and Gulf; local in much of the interior away from water.

Plate 30. **HAWKS 1 (VULTURES, EAGLES)**

Black
Vulture

Turkey
Vulture

Golden
Eagle

Bald
Eagle

Plate 31. HAWKS 2
(Buteos)

RED-TAILED HAWK — 23″
Reddish tail; white breast; dark streaks on belly. **Habitat:** Chiefly open country near woodlands—plains, prairies, deserts. **Range:** S. Canada to Mexican border; winter—withdraws from Canada, Montana, Dakotas. **Note:** This species is extremely variable, ranging from dark to very pale in color, but most adults may be told by reddish tails.

RED-SHOULDERED HAWK — 21″
Chestnut shoulders, body (below), and wing linings; tail with broad black bands and narrow white ones. **Habitat:** Wooded swamps, moist forests near rivers. **Range:** E. Nebraska, c. Kansas, w.c. parts of Oklahoma, Texas to Mexican border and Gulf; Pacific slope of California.

SWAINSON'S HAWK — 21″
Pale throat; dark breast; light-colored belly (white to reddish); light wing linings, dark flight feathers; in flight, tilts somewhat-pointed wings upward like a harrier; banded tail with broader band near tip. **Habitat:** Open country with scattered trees—plains, prairies, deserts. **Range:** Local from s. Canada to Mexican border; winters chiefly in s. South America. **Note:** Dark, almost blackish forms also occur.

ROUGH-LEGGED HAWK — 23″
Light phase—broad dark band near tip of white tail; dark patch at bend of mostly white wing; dark belly; dark phase—mainly black, but with much white in wing and tail from below. **Habitat:** Fields, prairies, plains, marshes, coastal areas. **Range:** Winters from s. Canada to Mexican border, but rare in s. parts from California east to Texas.

FERRUGINOUS HAWK — 24″
Rufous back and shoulders; whitish or pale head and tail; tail suffused with rusty; in flight from below—mainly white; chestnut legs, when folded, form a conspicuous **V**, evident when bird is overhead. **Habitat:** Dry open country, chiefly Great Plains, but also ranches and desert areas in winter. **Range:** Washington, s. parts of Alberta, Saskatchewan, North Dakota to w. portions of Nebraska, Kansas, Oklahoma, Texas, south to Mexican border; winters north to s.c. Oregon, c. Nevada, n.e. Utah, s.e. Wyoming, s.w. South Dakota.

Plate 31. **HAWKS 2 (BUTEOS)**

Red-tailed
Hawk

Red-shouldered
Hawk

Swainson's
Hawk

dark phase

light phase

Rough-legged
Hawk

Ferruginous
Hawk

71

Plate 32. HAWKS 3
(Accipiters, Osprey, Harrier)

SHARP-SHINNED HAWK — 12″

Short, rounded wings; long tail; blue-gray above, rusty-red below; flies with several flaps and a glide. **Habitat:** Woodlands, thickets. **Range:** S. Canada to Mexican border; winters north to Washington, s. Idaho, Wyoming, s.e. Nebraska.

NORTHERN GOSHAWK — 23″

Long, rounded wings; long tail; blue-gray above, pearl-gray below; conspicuous whitish line over eye. **Habitat:** Heavy coniferous and mixed forests; montane forests in s. portions of range; more open areas in winter. **Range:** S. Canada to mountains of n. Mexico; rare to absent east of Rockies, s. California, most of Texas.

OSPREY — 24″

Dark above, light below; black patch at bend of wings; dark facial patch. **Habitat:** Seacoasts, lakes, rivers. **Range:** Local from s. Canada to Mexican border, but rare to absent in dry open country; winters n. to s. California, s. Texas.

NORTHERN HARRIER (MARSH HAWK) — M 19″; F 22″

White rump; long wings and tail; male—pearl-gray above, pale below; female—brown above, streaked below; immature—rusty below, no streaks. **Habitat:** Marshes, fields, shores, beaches, prairies. **Range:** S. Canada to Mexican border; winters locally north to coast of s. British Columbia, inland to s. parts of Wyoming, Nebraska.

Plate 32. **HAWKS 3 (ACCIPITERS, OSPREY, HARRIER)**

Osprey

Sharp-shinned
Hawk

ad.

imm.

Northern
Goshawk

Northern
Harrier (Marsh Hawk)

F.

M.

Plate 33. HAWKS 4
(Kites, Falcons)

MISSISSIPPI KITE — 14″

Falcon-shaped with long *black* tail; long, pointed wings with black flight feathers; whitish rectangular patch at rear end of wings; head whitish; dark gray back and shoulders; pearl-gray below. **Habitat:** Open woodlands near water; prairies, plains with scattered trees (savannas). **Range:** Texas, Oklahoma, Kansas west to s.e. Colorado, New Mexico, e.c. Arizona, south to Mexican border; winters in tropics.

BLACK-SHOULDERED KITE — 16″

Falcon-shaped with long *white* tail; long, pointed wings with dark flight feathers (below) and *black* shoulders (above); white underparts, including head and wing linings; pearl-gray back. **Habitat:** Savannas, grasslands; ranches; marshes; along rivers and estuaries. **Range:** W. Oregon, most of California to Mexican border; southernmost Texas. **Note:** Often hovers over one spot—like a kestrel.

MERLIN — 12″

Long, pointed wings; heavily streaked below; banded tail; male—blue-gray above; female and immature—dark brown above. **Habitat:** Open country—beaches, fields, marshes, thickets, light woods. **Range:** S. Canada, northern tier of states south in mountains to Oregon, s. Idaho, Wyoming, Dakotas; winters along coast north to s. British Columbia, but inland only as far as the s. parts of Nevada, Arizona, New Mexico, Texas.

AMERICAN KESTREL — 11″

Long, pointed wings; reddish back and tail; blue-gray wings; black and white facial pattern; black band near tail tip; female—similar, but tail barred and wings reddish like back. **Habitat:** Open country—farms, fields, beaches, shores; cities. **Range:** S. Canada to Mexican border; winters along coast north to British Columbia, inland north to c. Idaho, s.w. Montana, s. Wyoming, n.e. Colorado, s. Nebraska.

PEREGRINE FALCON — 18″

Slaty-black above, buff below with dark bars; contrasting black and white face. **Habitat:** Open country with cliffs, especially near water; more rarely in cities with tall buildings; also bridges. **Range:** Local throughout, from s. Canada to Mexican border.

PRAIRIE FALCON — 18″

Light brown above, paler below with dark streaks and spots; narrow vertical patches on white face. Best field mark is *black* base and center of wing linings when bird is in overhead flight. **Habitat:** Dry open country with cliffs, canyons; buttes, mesas in deserts and plains. **Range:** S. Canada to Mexican border; winters north to s. portions of Washington, Idaho, Montana, Dakotas.

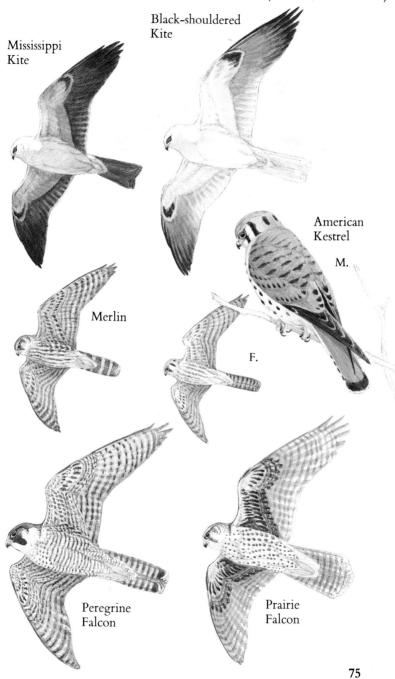

Plate 33. **HAWKS 4 (KITES, FALCONS)**

Mississippi
Kite

Black-shouldered
Kite

American
Kestrel

M.

Merlin

F.

Peregrine
Falcon

Prairie
Falcon

75

Plate 34. **SMALL OWLS**

ELF OWL — 5½″

Sparrow-sized—smallest owl in the world; very short tail; brownish over-all with indistinct rusty markings on white underparts. **Habitat:** Saguaro cactus deserts; oak and sycamore canyons. **Range:** Mainly c. and s. Arizona; s.w. New Mexico; local in w. and s. Texas; winters in Mexico.

NORTHERN PYGMY OWL — 7″

Long dark brown tail with narrow whitish bars; white-spotted crown and wings; black patches on each side of nape; white below with dark streaks; two color phases—brown and gray. **Habitat:** Open mixed montane forests, wooded canyons. **Range:** S. British Columbia, Alberta through Rockies to Mexican border; ranges southeast to e. parts of Colorado, New Mexico.

SAW-WHET OWL — 8″

Short tail; streaked forehead; white below with reddish-brown streaks. **Habitat:** Thick coniferous and mixed forests; winter—evergreen groves, thickets. **Range:** S. Canada to Mexican border, but farther east only to c. Texas. **Note:** Very tame—can sometimes be taken alive by hand!

WESTERN SCREECH OWL — 9″

Head tufts widely spaced; heavily mottled and streaked below; two color phases—dark brown and gray. **Habitat:** Open woods, farm groves, orchards; suburbs, city parks. **Range:** S. British Columbia, Washington, Idaho, w. Montana to Mexican border, east to w. Texas.

BURROWING OWL — 10″

Long legs; spotted forehead; white chin; barred below. **Habitat:** *Ground* owl of open country—grasslands, prairies, plains, deserts; also airports; often perches on fences, roadside wires. **Range:** Local from s. Canada to Mexican border and Gulf; winters north to c. California, s. Arizona, s.e. New Mexico, w.c. Texas.

Plate 34. **SMALL OWLS**

Elf
Owl

Northern
Pygmy Owl

Saw-whet Owl

Western
Screech Owl

Burrowing
Owl

Plate 35. LARGE OWLS

BARN OWL — 17″
White heart-shaped face; *dark* eyes; pale buff to cinnamon below with dots; rusty-brown above; long legs. **Habitat:** Chiefly open country—cliffs; large hollow trees; old buildings, silos, water towers, lighthouses; city parks. **Range:** U.S./Canada border to Mexican border and Gulf; winters north to Washington, s. Idaho, Wyoming, s. South Dakota.

SPOTTED OWL — 18″
Dark eyes; dark brown above and below, with creamy-white spots and blotches. **Habitat:** Thick forests—mainly conifers; also hardwoods in canyons. **Range:** Local over much of range—(1) Pacific slope from s.w. British Columbia to s. California; (2) s. Rocky Mountains from s. Utah, c. Colorado through Arizona, New Mexico, extreme w. Texas to c. Mexico.

SHORT-EARED OWL — 15½″
Tawny-buff; heavily streaked below. **Habitat:** Fields, prairies, plains, marshes, beaches; also airports, refuse dumps. **Range:** S. Canada to Mexican border; winters north to U.S./Canada border.

LONG-EARED OWL — 15″
Head tufts close together; streaked and mottled below. **Habitat:** Forests, thickets; winter—conifer groves. **Range:** S. Canada to Mexican border, but farther east only to c. Texas.

GREAT HORNED OWL — 22″
Head tufts widely spaced; white throat; finely barred below. **Habitat:** Extremely adaptable—from heavy forests, woodlots, swamps, and river bottoms to rocky deserts, cliffs, and canyons; even in large trees in city parks. **Range:** Widely distributed—from s. Canada to Mexican border and Gulf.

Plate 35. **LARGE OWLS**

Barn Owl

Spotted
Owl

Short-eared
Owl

Great Horned
Owl

Long-eared
Owl

Plate 36. **GEESE, SWANS**

CANADA GOOSE — 35″

Largest goose; long black neck and head; white chinstrap; light brown body. **Habitat:** Lakes, rivers, bays, inlets, marshes; grassy and cultivated (grain) fields. **Range:** S. Canada to Mexican border; winters along coast north to s. British Columbia, inland to s. parts of Oregon, Idaho, Wyoming, South Dakota.

BRANT — 25″

Small, Mallard-sized; short black neck and head; whitish below. **Habitat:** Bays, estuaries, salt marshes, tidal flats—essentially a marine goose. **Range:** Pacific Coast from British Columbia to Mexican border.

WHITE-FRONTED GOOSE — 30″

Medium-sized; grayish-brown with irregular black bars and blotches below; bill and legs pink to orange; at close range—white frontal band at base of bill, giving bird its name. **Habitat:** Mainly freshwater areas—lakes, marshes, flooded fields, grasslands. **Range:** Local from s. Canada to Mexican border; winters chiefly in Pacific States, also in small portions of Idaho, Montana, Wyoming, Utah, e. New Mexico, s. Texas; migrates nearly throughout.

SNOW GOOSE — 30″

Medium-sized; white phase—white with much black in wings; immature—pale gray; "blue" phase—dark grayish-brown with white head and upper neck. **Habitat:** Marshes, ponds, bays; cut-over grain fields. **Range:** S. Canada to Mexican border; winters chiefly in California, also locally in s. Arizona, e. New Mexico, s. Texas; migrates nearly throughout.

TUNDRA (WHISTLING) SWAN — 53″

All white; very long neck; black bill. **Habitat:** Lakes, rivers, bays, flooded fields. **Range:** Local from s. Canada to Mexican border; winters on Pacific Coast north to s. British Columbia, inland to s. Idaho, w. Utah, locally in s. Arizona, New Mexico, w. Texas.

TRUMPETER SWAN — 65″

Our largest waterfowl; similar to Tundra Swan but much larger; also heavier bill. **Habitat:** Chiefly inland lakes and marshes. **Range:** Sedentary—restricted in Canada to s. British Columbia, Alberta, s.w. Saskatchewan; in n.w. U.S. to Washington, s.e. Oregon, w. Montana, e. Idaho, n.w. Wyoming, South Dakota.

Plate 36. **GEESE, SWANS**

Canada Goose

Brant

White-fronted Goose

blue phase Snow Goose

in flight

Snow Goose white phase

Trumpeter Swan

Tundra (Whistling) Swan

81

Plate 37. TIPPING DUCKS 1

MALLARD — 24″
Bright green head; yellow bill; white neck ring; chestnut breast; blue wing patch bordered with white bars; female—mottled brown; orange bill with brown patch. **Habitat:** Marshes, ponds, lakes, rivers, bays, flooded fields. **Range:** S. Canada to Mexican border.

GADWALL — 21″
Dark gray; brown head and neck; small white wing patch, evident in flight. **Habitat:** Marshes, ponds, rivers. **Range:** S. Canada to Mexican border; winters along Pacific Coast north to s. British Columbia, inland to Idaho, s.e. Colorado, Kansas.

PINTAIL — 27″
White vertical line on side of dark brown head; white neck and breast; gray body; long, pointed tail. **Habitat:** Marshes, ponds, rivers. **Range:** S. Canada to Mexican border; winters north to s. British Columbia, w.c. Washington, s.w. Idaho, w. Utah, c. Colorado, s.e. Nebraska.

AMERICAN WIGEON (BALDPATE) — 20″
White crown; green head patch; *large* white wing patch, evident in flight. **Habitat:** Ponds, lakes, rivers, marshes, lagoons, bays, estuaries. **Range:** S. Canada to Mexican border; winters along Pacific Coast north to s. British Columbia, inland to s. Nevada, Arizona, s. New Mexico, w. and s. Texas.

FULVOUS WHISTLING DUCK — 19″
Tawny body; all-black wings, evident in flight. **Habitat:** Shallow water in marshes, lagoons, ricefields, estuaries. **Range:** Mexican border north to c. California, s.w. Arizona; also s. Texas along Gulf.

BLACK-BELLIED WHISTLING DUCK — 21″
Gray face and bright *reddish* bill; chestnut neck, breast, and back; black belly; pink legs; large white wing patch. **Habitat:** Wooded ponds, streams; marshes, lagoons. **Range:** S. portions of Arizona, Texas.

Plate 37. **TIPPING DUCKS 1**

M.

Mallard

F.

Gadwall

American Wigeon (Baldpate)

Pintail

Fulvous
Whistling Duck

Black-bellied
Whistling Duck

Plate 38. TIPPING DUCKS 2

GREEN-WINGED TEAL — 14"
Chestnut head with green patch; white vertical line in front of wing; gray body; green wing patch, evident in flight. **Habitat:** Marshes, ponds, estuaries. **Range:** S. Canada to Mexican border; winters north to coastal Washington, inland to c. Idaho, s.w. Montana, Wyoming, s.w. Nebraska.

BLUE-WINGED TEAL — 16"
White crescent behind bill; light blue wing patch, evident in flight. **Habitat:** Marshes, ponds, lagoons. **Range:** S. Canada to Mexican border; winters north only to c. California, s. Texas, otherwise south of border.

CINNAMON TEAL — 17"
Cinnamon-red head and body; light blue wing patch, evident in flight. **Habitat:** Marshes, ponds, lagoons. **Range:** S. parts of British Columbia, Alberta, Saskatchewan to Mexican border, east to w. edge of Great Plains; winters north to c. California, s. parts of Arizona, New Mexico, Texas.

SHOVELER — 20"
Long, shovel-shaped bill, pointed down; green head; white chest; chestnut sides; light blue wing patch, evident in flight. **Habitat:** Marshes, ponds, lagoons, estuaries. **Range:** S. Canada to Mexican border; winters north to Oregon, Nevada, Utah, c. New Mexico, Oklahoma

WOOD DUCK — 18½"
Gaudily colored in green, purple, blue, and white; chestnut breast; at close range—red eye and base of bill; swept-back crest; female—dull, mostly grayish; prominent white eye patch. **Habitat:** Swamps, marshes, wooded ponds, streams. **Range:** Local along Pacific Coast from s. British Columbia to Mexican border; inland from s. Manitoba, Washington, Oregon, c. Idaho, s.w. Montana, n. Wyoming, Dakotas to Arizona, c. Colorado, n.w. and s. New Mexico, Kansas, Oklahoma, nearly all of Texas; winters north to Washington, Arizona, New Mexico, c. Colorado, s.e. Kansas.

Plate 38. **TIPPING DUCKS 2**

Green-winged Teal

Blue-winged
Teal

Cinnamon Teal

Shoveler

F.

Wood Duck

M.

Plate 39. DIVING DUCKS 1

GREATER AND LESSER SCAUP — 18″ and 16½″
Black fore and aft; light in the middle; close up—profile only; head of
Greater, green; head of Lesser, purple; females—brownish, with distinct
white patch at base of bill; indistinguishable from each other on water.
Habitat: Lakes, rivers, bays, estuaries; Greater Scaup also on ocean and
Gulf. **Range:** Greater—S. British Columbia to Mexican border, restricted
mainly along Pacific Coast; rare and local inland. Lesser—S. Canada to
Mexican border; winters locally north along Pacific Coast to s. British
Columbia, inland to Great Basin area.

RING-NECKED DUCK — 16½″
Black head, back, and breast; white wedge in front of wing; pale gray sides;
pale blue bill with white ring and black tip; at close range—purplish gloss
on head. **Habitat:** Wooded ponds, lakes, rivers. **Range:** Local—Pacific
Coast from s. British Columbia to Mexican border; inland in s. Manitoba,
Dakotas, Washington, Oregon, n. California, n.w. Nevada; winters in s.
parts of Arizona, New Mexico, Texas, along Pacific Coast from s. British
Columbia to Mexican border.

REDHEAD — 20″
Gray body; reddish head; black chest; *rounded* profile; *short* bill. **Habitat:**
Lakes, rivers, marshes, bays, estuaries. **Range:** S. Canada to Mexican bor-
der; winters north to California, s. Nevada, Utah, Colorado, Kansas.

CANVASBACK — 22″
White body; chestnut head and neck; black chest; *sloping* profile; *long* bill.
Habitat: Lakes, rivers, marshes, bays, estuaries. **Range:** S. Canada to
Mexican border; winters north to British Columbia, Montana, w. South
Dakota.

Plate 39. **DIVING DUCKS 1**

Greater Scaup

Lesser Scaup F.

M.

Ring-necked Duck

Redhead

Canvasback

87

Plate 40. DIVING DUCKS 2

BUFFLEHEAD — 14″

Large white patch on dark head; white body; black back; close up—iridescent green and purple head; female—small white patch on dark head behind eye; grayish body. **Habitat:** Lakes, rivers, bays, inlets, estuaries. **Range:** S. Canada to Mexican border; winters north to British Columbia, Nevada, s.w. Utah, New Mexico, s.e. Nebraska.

COMMON GOLDENEYE — 18″

Dark puffy head; white body; white patch behind bill; black back; close up—glossy *green* head; bright yellow eye; female—gray body and dark brown head separated by white collar. **Habitat:** Lakes, rivers, bays, inlets, estuaries. **Range:** Pacific Coast from British Columbia to Mexican border; also s.e. California, s.w. Arizona.

BARROW'S GOLDENEYE — 18″

White crescent between bill and eye; close up—glossy *purple* head; black back with row of white spots along side; white below. **Habitat:** Wooded lakes, ponds, rivers; inlets, estuaries. **Range:** Pacific Coast from British Columbia to c. California, inland from Washington, Oregon to n. Idaho, w. Montana, n.w. Wyoming; winters south to Utah, Colorado; also s.e. California, s. Arizona.

HOODED MERGANSER — 17½″

Fan-shaped white crest with black border; rusty sides; white breast with two vertical black stripes; black face, neck, and back. **Habitat:** Wooded lakes, ponds, streams. **Range:** S. British Columbia to Mexican border; winters inland to n. Idaho, s. Oregon, s.e. California, s.w. Arizona.

RED-BREASTED MERGANSER — 23″

Swept-back double crest; red bill; white collar; rusty chest; black back. **Habitat:** Chiefly coastal waters, including ocean. **Range:** Pacific Coast from British Columbia to Mexican border; also s.e. California, extreme s. Nevada, s.w. Arizona.

COMMON MERGANSER — 25″

Dark, glossy green head; red bill; white body; black back; female—duller, with red head. **Habitat:** Lakes, reservoirs, rivers; bays in winter. **Range:** S. Canada to Mexican border; winters north to coast of British Columbia, inland to n.e. Oregon, c. Idaho, Wyoming, Dakotas, rarely to s.e. Saskatchewan, s.w. Manitoba.

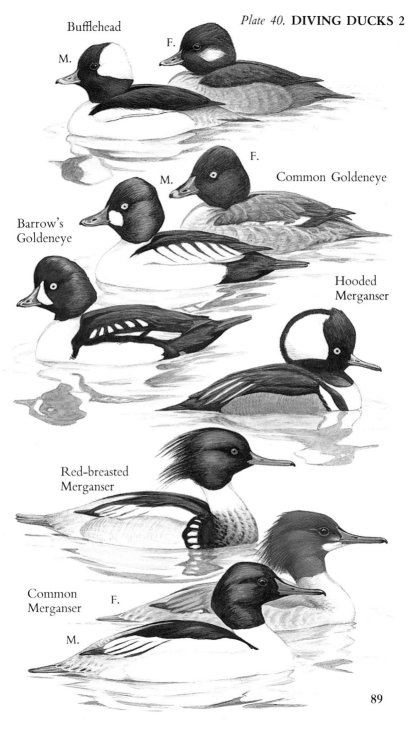

Plate 40. **DIVING DUCKS 2**

Bufflehead

M.

F.

Common Goldeneye

M.

F.

Barrow's
Goldeneye

Hooded
Merganser

Red-breasted
Merganser

Common
Merganser

F.

M.

89

Plate 41. **DIVING DUCKS 3**

RUDDY DUCK — 15½″
White cheek; bright blue bill; chestnut body; dark cap; cocks tail up into a fan; female—much duller, white cheek with dark horizontal stripe. **Habitat:** Marshes, ponds, lakes, bays, lagoons, estuaries. **Range:** S. Canada to Mexican border; winters along coast north to British Columbia, but inland only to Arizona, New Mexico, c. Texas.

HARLEQUIN DUCK — 16½″
Slaty head; blue-gray chest and back; prominent white markings on head and body; chestnut sides; female—dusky-brown; *three* white facial patches. **Habitat:** Summer—montane streams in forested areas; winter—rocky coasts. **Range:** S. British Columbia to Washington, n.e. Oregon, c. Idaho, w. Montana, n.w. Wyoming; winters along coast from s. British Columbia to c. California.

BLACK SCOTER — 18″
All-black sea duck; large orange knob on black bill. **Habitat:** Ocean, bays, large lakes, rivers. **Range:** Pacific Coast from British Columbia to Mexican border.

SURF SCOTER — 19″
Black sea duck; two white head patches—one on forecrown, one on nape; bill black, white, yellow, and reddish. **Habitat:** Ocean, bays, large lakes, rivers. **Range:** Pacific Coast from British Columbia to Mexican border.

WHITE-WINGED SCOTER — 21″
Black sea duck; small white eye patch; larger white wing patch, most evident in flight; orange bill with black basal knob. **Habitat:** Ocean, bays, large lakes, rivers. **Range:** S. Canada to Mexican border; winters along Pacific Coast. **Note:** All three scoters are rare and irregular *inland* in western United States.

Plate 41. **DIVING DUCKS 3**

Ruddy Duck

F.

M. summer

Harlequin Duck

F.

M.

Black Scoter

Surf Scoter

White-winged Scoter

91

Plate 42. ALCIDS, LOONS

PIGEON GUILLEMOT — 13″

Small chunky seabird; pointed bill; mostly black; large white wing patch with triangular black wedge; red feet; winter—white head, neck, and below. **Habitat:** Rocky coasts, islands, ocean. **Range:** Pacific Coast from s. British Columbia to Mexican border.

THIN-BILLED (COMMON) MURRE — 17″

Stocky seabird; long, *slender,* pointed bill; deep sooty-brown above, white below; winter—similar, but neck and throat white; black cheek stripe. **Habitat:** Rocky coasts, islands; ocean. **Range:** Pacific Coast from s. British Columbia to Mexican border.

RED-THROATED LOON — 25″

Sharp, pointed bill tilted *upward;* nonbreeding plumage—white head, neck, and below. **Habitat:** Ocean, bays, estuaries. **Range:** Pacific Coast from s. British Columbia to Mexican border. **Note:** Rarely seen in breeding plumage (red throat).

ARCTIC (PACIFIC) LOON — 25″

Sharp, pointed, *straight* bill; pearl-gray crown and nape; black throat; conspicuous square white patches on dark back; winter—white cheeks and throat; dark line from eye down side of neck. **Habitat:** Ocean. **Range:** Pacific Coast from s. British Columbia to Mexican border.

COMMON LOON — 32″

Large size; long, sharp, pointed, *straight* bill; black head and neck; blotched black and white back and sides; winter—white face, neck, and below. **Habitat:** Large wooded lakes, ocean, bays. **Range:** S. Canada, Pacific Coast from Washington to Mexican border; occasionally inland in winter to s.e. California, s.w. Arizona.

Pigeon Guillemot

winter

summer

winter

summer

Thin-billed (Common) Murre

Red-throated Loon

winter

winter

Arctic (Pacific) Loon

summer

Common Loon

winter

summer

Plate 42. **ALCIDS, LOONS**

93

Plate 43. GREBES

PIED-BILLED GREBE — 13″

Black ring on thick whitish bill; brownish body with black throat; non-breeding—similar but *no* black. **Habitat:** Marshes, weedy ponds, lakes; bays in winter. **Range:** S. Canada to Mexican border; winters north to s. British Columbia, Nevada, Utah, s.w. Colorado, s. Kansas.

HORNED GREBE — 13½″

Golden ear tufts; black head and back; *chestnut* neck and sides; nonbreeding—black above, white below. **Habitat:** Lakes, ponds, rivers, bays, inlets, ocean. **Range:** Chiefly Pacific Coast from British Columbia to Mexican border; also s. Canada and n. U.S. border states, but in winter only along coast and extreme s. Texas.

EARED GREBE — 13″

Golden ear tufts; *black* head, *neck,* chest, and back; chestnut below; non-breeding—blackish above with white only on chin and small patch behind cheek; thin, upturned bill. **Habitat:** Ponds, lakes, bays, ocean. **Range:** S. Canada to Mexican border; winters along Pacific Coast, inland north to Nevada, Utah, Colorado, c. Texas.

WESTERN GREBE — 25″

Our largest grebe; extremely long, swan-like neck; black above, white below; long, thin, slightly upturned bill; in northern form—bill *greenish;* black cap extends *below* eye; in southern form—bill *yellow-orange;* white cheek *surrounds* eye. **Habitat:** Reedy lakes, ponds; bays, estuaries. **Range:** Local along entire coast from s.w. British Columbia to Mexican border; *all* of California; s.e. Saskatchewan, s. Manitoba to Dakotas; in most Mountain States, but only s.w. Arizona; also w. and s. Texas. **Note:** Two different species are involved. The two forms are reported *not* to interbreed. The more southern species is known as Clark's Grebe.

Plate 43. **GREBES**

Pied-billed
Grebe

winter

Horned
Grebe

summer

Eared
Grebe

summer

winter

Clark's
Grebe

Western
Grebe

95

Plate 44. RAILS, GALLINULE, COOT

SORA — 9″

Chicken-like; short, thick yellow bill; black face, throat, and chest; brown above, gray below; narrow white bars on flanks. **Habitat:** Marshes, moist meadows. **Range:** S. Canada to Mexican border; winters north to Washington, s. Nevada, c. Arizona, New Mexico, Texas.

VIRGINIA RAIL — 9½″

Chicken-like; long, slender, slightly curved bill; grayish-brown above; gray cheeks; rusty below; large chestnut wing patch; narrow white bars on gray flanks. **Habitat:** Marshes. **Range:** Local from s. Canada to Mexican border, c. New Mexico, n. Texas, much of Oklahoma; winters north to Washington, s. Nevada, Arizona, c. New Mexico, lower Gulf Coast of s. Texas.

CLAPPER/KING RAIL — 15″

Chicken-like; much larger than Virginia Rail; long, slender, slightly curved bill; grayish-brown above; cheeks and breast vary from gray to rusty; narrow white bars on flanks. **Habitat:** Coastal and inland marshes. **Range:** Local from c. and s. California to s.w. Arizona; lower Gulf Coast of s. Texas. **Note:** The Clapper/King Rail complex is here treated as a single species. Vocalizations are virtually identical. The former is found in California and s.w. Arizona; the latter occurs only in s. Texas.

COMMON GALLINULE (MOORHEN) — 13″

Bright red forehead and bill with yellow tip; deep gray head and body; olive-brown back; narrow white side stripe. **Habitat:** Marshes, ponds; lawns near water. **Range:** Local—resident from c. California, s.w. Nevada, c. Arizona, c. New Mexico to Mexican border; also Oklahoma, e.c. Texas.

AMERICAN COOT — 14½″

Deep gray with *white* bill. **Habitat:** Marshes, ponds, lakes, bays; lawns, fields. **Range:** S. Canada to Mexican border; winters north to s. British Columbia, n.e. Nevada, s. Utah, s. and e. Colorado, most of Nebraska.

Sora

Plate 44. **RAILS, GALLINULE, COOT**

Virginia Rail

Clapper /King Rail

Common Gallinule (Moorhen)

American Coot

97

Plate 45. CORMORANTS, PELICANS

BRANDT'S CORMORANT — 34″
All black with blue chin pouch, bordered behind with buff. **Habitat:** Cliffs along rocky seacoasts. **Range:** Pacific Coast from British Columbia to Mexican border.

PELAGIC CORMORANT — 27″
All black with green and purple iridescence at close range; white flank patch in breeding adult, evident in flight. **Habitat:** Cliffs along rocky seacoasts. **Range:** Pacific Coast from British Columbia to Mexican border.

DOUBLE-CRESTED CORMORANT — 33″
All black with orange chin pouch. **Habitat:** Coastal bays, islands; inland lakes, rivers. **Range:** Resident on Pacific Coast from British Columbia to Mexican border; Rio Grande and Gulf Coast of Texas; breeds from s. Canada south through much of inland states to Utah, Colorado, Dakotas, Nebraska, but winters north only to U.S./Mexican border and Lower Gulf.

BROWN PELICAN — 50″
Very large; grayish-brown; very long grayish-white bill; white head, chestnut neck; immature—dull brownish. **Habitat:** Ocean, bays, inlets, beaches. **Range:** C. California to Mexican border; less common north along coast to Washington.

WHITE PELICAN — 62″
Huge white bird; very long orange bill; much black in wings, evident in flight. **Habitat:** Lakes, marshes, shallow bays, coastal estuaries. **Range:** Breeds locally on large inland lakes from s. Canada to Mexican border; winters locally north to c. California, s. Nevada, w. Arizona, extreme s. Texas.

Plate 45. **CORMORANTS, PELICANS**

Brandt's
Cormorant

Pelagic Cormorant

Double-
crested
Cormorant

Brown
Pelican

in flight

White
Pelican

Plate 46. **LONG-LEGGED WADERS 1**

CATTLE EGRET — 20″
Stocky and thick-necked; breeding—golden-buff plumes on head, breast, and back; short orange-red bill; reddish legs; nonbreeding—all-white plumage; yellow bill; greenish legs. **Habitat:** Fields, pastures, farms; airports; golf courses, lawns. **Range:** S. portions of California, Arizona, New Mexico; South Dakota to Texas; wanders north to U.S./Canada border; winters primarily along U.S./Mexican border and in much of Texas. **Note:** Often associates with cattle and other livestock.

SNOWY EGRET — 23″
All-white plumage; black bill and legs; yellow feet. **Habitat:** Marshes, swamps, ponds, shallow bays, tidal flats. **Range:** S. parts of Oregon, Idaho, Wyoming to Mexican border, east to c. Colorado, Oklahoma, w. Texas; wanders north to U.S./Canada border; winters north to n. California, s. Nevada, w. Arizona, extreme s. Texas.

GREAT EGRET — 38″
All-white plumage; yellow bill; black legs. **Habitat:** Marshes, swamps, ponds, bays, tidal flats. **Range:** Oregon to Mexican border; s. Arizona, New Mexico; also s.e. Kansas, e.c. Oklahoma to c. Texas; wanders north to U.S./Canada border; winters north to s.w. Oregon, s. Nevada, s. Arizona, s.w. New Mexico, extreme s. Texas.

GREAT BLUE HERON — 44″
Very large; bluish-gray; whitish head; black head plumes. **Habitat:** Marshes, swamps, lakes, rivers, bays, estuaries. **Range:** S. Canada to Mexican border; winters north to s. British Columbia, e. Oregon, Nevada, s. Utah, s.w. Colorado, c. Oklahoma. **Note:** Flies with neck *folded in.*

SANDHILL CRANE — 45″
Very large; all-gray plumage; bare red crown; black legs. **Habitat:** Prairies, fields, swales, marshes. **Range:** Local from s. Alberta, Saskatchewan to e. Washington, Oregon, n. Nevada, Idaho, w. Montana, Wyoming, extreme n. Utah, Colorado; winters in c. and s.e. California, s. parts of Arizona, New Mexico, w., c., and s. Texas. **Note:** Flies with neck *outstretched.*

Plate 46. **LONG-LEGGED WADERS 1**

summer

Cattle
Egret

winter

Great
Egret

Snowy
Egret

in flight

Sandhill
Crane

Great Blue
Heron

in flight

101

Plate 47. LONG-LEGGED WADERS 2

LEAST BITTERN — 13″

Our smallest heron; greenish-black above; buff wing patch; tawny sides of head and neck. **Habitat:** Dense marshes, especially those with cattails and tulé. **Range:** Local in West—from c. California to Mexican border; s.w. Arizona; from Dakotas south to c. and s.w. Texas; winters chiefly south of border, rarely in s. California, s. Arizona, lower Gulf Coast of s. Texas.

AMERICAN BITTERN — 23″

Stocky; tawny-brown with dark streaks below—blending with reeds; black neck stripe; blackish outer wings, evident in flight. **Habitat:** Marshes, wet meadows, bogs. **Range:** S. Canada to Mexican border; winters north along Pacific Coast to s.w. British Columbia, inland to s. parts of Nevada, Utah, n. New Mexico, w. and c. Texas.

GREEN-BACKED HERON — 18″

Small and chunky; chestnut head and neck; bluish-gray back and wings, the back with a green sheen; greenish-yellow legs. **Habitat:** Marshes, swamps, wooded ponds, streams, coastal thickets. **Range:** Local from s. Canada to Mexican border; winters north to California, s. Arizona, extreme s. Texas.

BLACK-CROWNED NIGHT HERON — 25″

Stocky; black cap and back; two long white head plumes in breeding season; gray wings; white below; immature—brown, streaked and spotted with white. **Habitat:** Marshes, swamps, wooded ponds, streams, tidal flats. **Range:** Local from s. Canada to Mexican border; winters north to s.w. Oregon, s.w. Arizona, extreme s. Texas.

WHITE-FACED IBIS — 24″

Black at distance; slender, decurved bill; close up—iridescent bronze-green, chestnut and purple. Very similar to Glossy Ibis of the East, but has *white* border nearly around red eye and red facial skin; reddish bill and legs. **Habitat:** Marshes, swamps, coastal estuaries. **Range:** Local—c. California, s.e. Oregon, Nevada, Utah, e. portions of Rocky Mountain States from s.e. Montana, Dakotas, Colorado, New Mexico, Texas; from Nebraska to e.c. parts of Kansas, Oklahoma; winters in s. Texas, otherwise south of Mexican border.

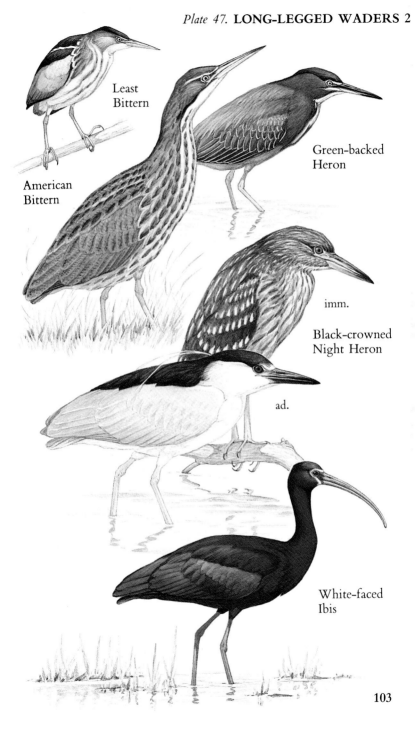

Plate 47. **LONG-LEGGED WADERS 2**

Least
Bittern

American
Bittern

Green-backed
Heron

imm.

Black-crowned
Night Heron

ad.

White-faced
Ibis

Plate 48. LARGE SHOREBIRDS

BLACK-NECKED STILT — 15″
Black above, white below; long red legs; thin black bill. **Habitat:** Open marshes, shallow lakes, pools; tidal flats and estuaries. **Range:** Local from Oregon, Nevada, Utah, s. Colorado, w.c. Kansas to Mexican border; winters chiefly south of border, but also s. parts of California, Arizona, Texas.

AMERICAN AVOCET — 18″
Flashy black and white wings; long, slender, upturned black bill; blue-gray legs; head and neck in breeding plumage—rusty; nonbreeding—pale gray. **Habitat:** Shallow lakes, open marshes, shores, flats. **Range:** S. Alberta, Saskatchewan, Manitoba to Mexican border, east to Dakotas, c. Nebraska, w. Kansas, w. Oklahoma, n.w. Texas; winters in w.c. and s.e. California, s. Arizona, extreme s. Texas.

MARBLED GODWIT — 18″
Long, slightly upturned bill; tawny-brown body. **Habitat:** Prairies; pools, lake shores; coastal flats, beaches. **Range:** Breeds locally from s. Alberta, Saskatchewan, Manitoba to Montana, Dakotas; migrates throughout much of West; winters chiefly south of U.S./Mexican border, but also along Pacific Coast of California, Gulf Coast of Texas.

LONG-BILLED CURLEW — 23″
Our largest shorebird; extremely long, decurved bill; cinnamon-brown above, tawny-buff below. **Habitat:** Plains, prairies, wet meadows, shores, beaches. **Range:** Local from s. Canada to Mexican border; east to w. Dakotas, n.w. Nebraska, e. Colorado, n.e. New Mexico, Texas; winters locally in California, s.w. Arizona, c. and s. Texas.

WHIMBREL — 17″
Long, decurved bill; brown and white head stripes; gray-brown body. **Habitat:** Shores, flats, prairies, wet meadows. **Range:** Breeds locally in high Arctic; migrates nearly throughout; winters chiefly in tropics, but also along Pacific Coast of California, Gulf Coast of Texas.

Plate 48. **LARGE SHOREBIRDS**

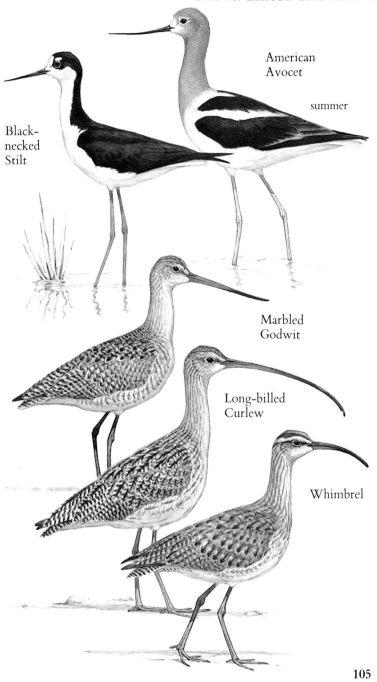

American
Avocet

summer

Black-
necked
Stilt

Marbled
Godwit

Long-billed
Curlew

Whimbrel

Plate 49. MEDIUM SHOREBIRDS

SPOTTED SANDPIPER — 7½″

Breeding—black spots below; nonbreeding—plain white below; white wedge in front of wing; rear end teeters up and down; in flight, flutters stiffly held, downcurved wings. **Habitat:** Shores of ponds, streams, often on logs, rocks; beaches, dunes. **Range:** S. Canada to Mexican border; winters along West Coast north to Washington, inland to c. California, s. Arizona, s. New Mexico, c. Texas.

UPLAND SANDPIPER — 12″

Tawny-brown; thin neck; long tail; yellowish legs. **Habitat:** Short-grass prairies, hayfields, meadows, pastures; airports; often perches on poles, fence posts. **Range:** Very local—breeds from s. Alberta, Saskatchewan, Manitoba; from e. Washington, Idaho, Montana, North Dakota to e. Wyoming, south to n.e. Colorado, n.w. Oklahoma; migrates mainly through w. plains, prairies; winters in South America.

COMMON SNIPE — 11″

Extremely long bill; striped head and back; tawny-orange tail, evident in flight. **Habitat:** Bogs, marshes, flooded fields, meadows. **Range:** S. Canada to Mexican border; winters north along w. coast to s. British Columbia, inland to s.e. Oregon, s. Idaho, Colorado, n.e. New Mexico, c. Texas.

LONG-BILLED DOWITCHER — 11–12″

Extremely long bill; breeding—rusty-red breast with black spots; sides with bars; nonbreeding—dull gray; white eye stripe; all year—conspicuous white rump wedge, evident in flight. **Habitat:** Tidal flats, muddy shores, open marshes, grassy pools, lagoons. **Range:** Breeds in far north; migrates along West Coast, inland from s. Canada to Mexican border; winters north along coast to British Columbia, inland along U.S./Mexican border, Gulf Coast. **Note:** Feeds in mud and fairly deep water, using its long bill in "sewing-machine rhythm."

GREATER YELLOWLEGS — 14″

Bright yellow legs; long bill; bobs up and down; white rump in flight. **Habitat:** Tidal flats, marshes, lake and river shores, flooded fields; golf courses. **Range:** S. Canada to Mexican border; migrates throughout; winters along coast north to Washington, inland to s. Nevada, c. Arizona, n.e. New Mexico, w. and s. Texas.

WILLET — 15″

Flashy black and white wings in flight; bluish-gray legs; breeding—speckled body; nonbreeding—pale gray, unmarked. **Habitat:** Marshes, meadows, tidal flats, shores, beaches. **Range:** S. Canada to Mexican border; migrates throughout; winters along Pacific and Gulf coasts, north to Oregon.

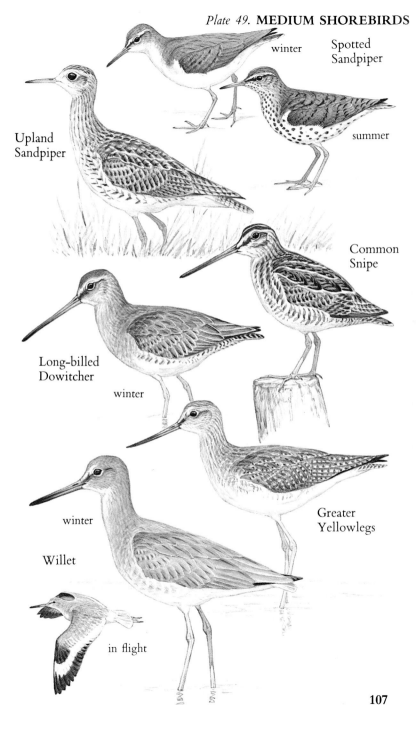

Plate 49. **MEDIUM SHOREBIRDS**

winter

Spotted
Sandpiper

Upland
Sandpiper

summer

Common
Snipe

Long-billed
Dowitcher

winter

winter

Greater
Yellowlegs

Willet

in flight

Plate 50. SMALL SHOREBIRDS

WESTERN SANDPIPER — 6½″
Black legs; bill with slight droop at tip; reddish feathers at bend of wing (scapulars). **Habitat:** Shores, mud flats, beaches. **Range:** Breeds in high Arctic; migrates throughout; winters north along Pacific Coast to n. California, inland to s.w. Arizona, Gulf Coast of s. Texas.

LEAST SANDPIPER — 5½″
Our smallest shorebird; greenish-yellow legs; heavily streaked breast. **Habitat:** Grassy mud flats, pools, marsh edges. **Range:** Breeds in high Arctic; migrates throughout; winters north to coast of Oregon, inland to s. Nevada, c. parts of Arizona, New Mexico, Texas.

DUNLIN — 8½″
Bill droops at tip; breeding—black patch on belly; reddish back; nonbreeding—grayish-brown above, whitish below. **Habitat:** Tidal flats, shores, beaches. **Range:** Breeds in high Arctic; migrates mainly along coast, less common inland; winters north along coast to British Columbia, inland to s.w. Arizona, Gulf Coast of extreme s. Texas.

SANDERLING — 7½″
Breeding—rusty head, back, and breast; nonbreeding—our palest sandpiper, appearing almost white in flight. **Habitat:** Ocean beaches, sand flats, shores. **Range:** Breeds in high Arctic; migrates throughout, but most prevalent along both coasts; winters north along Pacific Coast to British Columbia, Gulf Coast of Texas. **Note:** Frequents outer sand beaches, running in and out of waves.

RED KNOT — 10½″
Greenish legs; breeding—brick-red below; nonbreeding—gray above, whitish below. **Habitat:** Tidal flats, shores, beaches, salt meadows. **Range:** Breeds in high Arctic; migrates chiefly along coasts, much less common inland; winters north to c. California, extreme s. Texas.

WILSON'S PHALAROPE — 9″
Long, thin, needle-like bill; breeding—black stripe through eye, extending down neck; cinnamon below black stripe, curving to back; pale gray crown and nape; nonbreeding—combination of white rump in flight and pale unmarked wings and body. **Habitat:** Shallow lakes, ponds; marshes; short-grass flats. **Range:** Breeds from s. Canada to c. California, Nevada, Utah, Colorado, w. Kansas; migrates throughout; winters in South America.

RED-NECKED PHALAROPE — 8″
Breeding—chestnut sides and front of neck; white throat; mostly gray above; nonbreeding—pale gray and white with prominent black patch behind eye; striped back. **Habitat:** Coastal lagoons, estuaries; less numerous on inland lakes. **Range:** Breeds in high Arctic; migrates along coasts, much less numerous inland; winters at sea. **Note:** Phalaropes frequently spin around in the water.

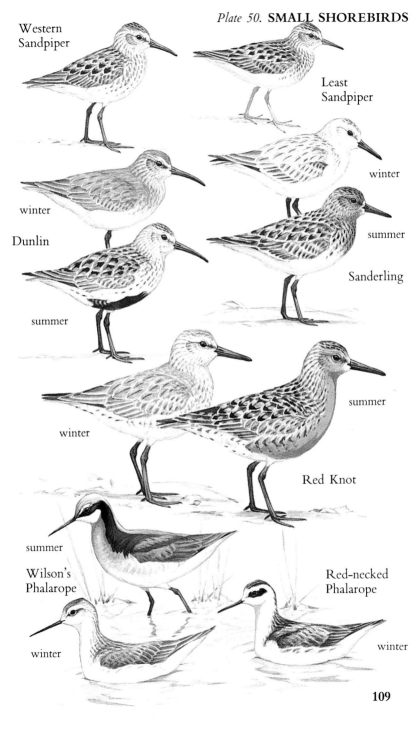

Plate 50. **SMALL SHOREBIRDS**

Western
Sandpiper

Least
Sandpiper

winter

Dunlin

winter

summer

Sanderling

summer

winter

summer

Red Knot

summer

Wilson's
Phalarope

Red-necked
Phalarope

winter

winter

109

Plate 51. **ROCK-LOVING SHOREBIRDS**

RUDDY TURNSTONE — 9″

Orange legs; breeding—striking black, white, and reddish plumage; non-breeding—much duller, brownish above, white below with dark breast patch. **Habitat:** Rocky shores, islands, pebbly beaches, tidal flats, salt meadows. **Range:** Breeds in high Arctic; migrates chiefly along coasts, rare in interior; winters north to s.w. Oregon; extreme s. Texas.

BLACK TURNSTONE — 9″

Blackish legs; mostly black, with white belly; striking black and white wing and tail pattern, evident in flight. **Habitat:** Rocky shores, jetties, pebbly beaches, flats. **Range:** On the coast from British Columbia to Mexican border.

SURFBIRD — 10″

Nonbreeding only—stocky with heavy, short bill; slaty above; paler breast and whitish belly; greenish legs; in flight, striking white rump and base of tail, with black triangular tail band. **Habitat:** Rocky shores, jetties. **Range:** Winters on Pacific Coast from s. British Columbia to Mexican border.

ROCK SANDPIPER — 8½″

Dark bill with light base, slightly downcurved; nonbreeding only—slaty above; pale gray breast, white belly; greenish-yellow legs. **Habitat:** Rocky shores, jetties. **Range:** Winters on Pacific Coast from s. British Columbia to n. California. **Note:** Similar in appearance and habitat to Purple Sandpiper of Atlantic Coast.

WANDERING TATTLER — 11″

Nonbreeding only—uniform slaty above, paler below; yellowish legs; in flight, *no* markings on solid gray wings or tail. **Habitat:** Rocky shores, jetties. **Range:** Migrates along Pacific Coast from s. British Columbia to Mexican border; winters north to s. California, rarely farther.

BLACK OYSTERCATCHER — 17½″

Large; all-black plumage; heavy red bill; flesh-colored legs. **Habitat:** Rocky coasts, islands, stone jetties. **Range:** Resident along Pacific Coast from s. British Columbia to Mexican border.

Plate 51. **ROCK-LOVING SHOREBIRDS**

winter

Ruddy
Turnstone

summer

winter

Black
Turnstone

summer

Surfbird

winter

Rock Sandpiper

winter

Wandering
Tattler

winter

Black
Oystercatcher

111

Plate 52. MORE SHOREBIRDS—PLOVERS

SEMIPALMATED PLOVER — 7″

Single black breast band; dark above, white below; yellow bill with black tip; yellow legs. **Habitat:** Mud flats, beaches, lake and river shores. **Range:** Breeds in high Arctic; migrates throughout; winters along coasts, north to c. California, s. Texas.

SNOWY PLOVER — 6½″

No breast band; pale above, white below; dark patches on crown, behind eye, and on side of breast; thin black bill; slaty legs. **Habitat:** Sand beaches, flats; alkaline lake and river shores. **Range:** Local along Pacific Coast from s.w. Washington to Mexican border; inland from s. Oregon, to s.e. California, s. Arizona, s.e. New Mexico, and from s.w. to n.c. Kansas, Gulf Coast, and s. Texas.

KILLDEER — 10″

Two black breast bands; brown above, white below; tawny-orange rump, evident in flight. **Habitat:** Short-grass and plowed fields; airports; golf courses; lake and river shores. **Range:** S. Canada to Mexican border; winters on coast north to British Columbia, inland to n. California, s. Nevada, Arizona, New Mexico, Oklahoma, s.e. Kansas.

MOUNTAIN PLOVER — 9″

Dark above, white below—our only plover which is *unmarked* below. **Habitat:** Semiarid country on high plains, plateaus, short-grass fields, barren desert flats—often far from water. **Range:** Breeds locally from s. Alberta, Saskatchewan through Montana, Wyoming, Colorado, n.e. New Mexico, more rarely to w. portions of Nebraska, Kansas, Oklahoma, Texas; winters from Mexican border north to California, s. Arizona, extreme s. Texas.

GOLDEN PLOVER — 10½″

Breeding—all black below, dark above with golden spangles; white forehead over and behind eye, and down neck; nonbreeding—dark above, lighter below; *dark* rump. **Habitat:** Prairies; short-grass, plowed fields. **Range:** Breeds in high Arctic; migrates throughout; winters in s. South America.

BLACK-BELLIED PLOVER — 12″

Breeding—black below with white vent; mottled gray and white above; white forehead over and behind eye, and down neck; nonbreeding— whitish below; *white* rump, evident in flight. **Habitat:** Tidal flats, salt meadows, shores; plowed fields; golf courses; large lawns. **Range:** Breeds in high Arctic; migrates throughout; winters along Pacific Coast from British Columbia to Mexican border; lower Gulf Coast of Texas.

Plate 52. **MORE SHOREBIRDS—PLOVERS**

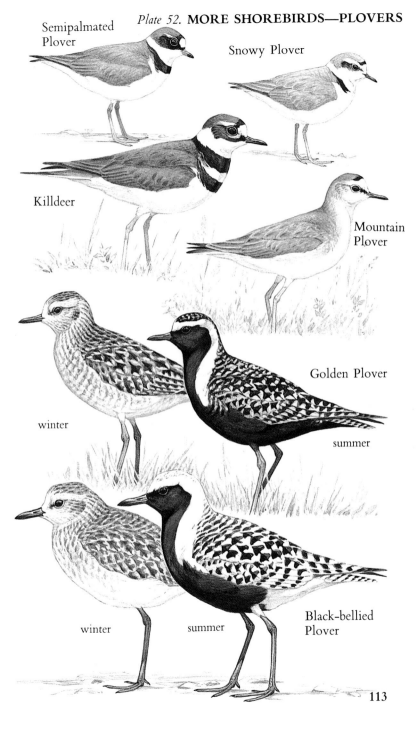

Semipalmated Plover

Snowy Plover

Killdeer

Mountain Plover

Golden Plover

winter

summer

winter

summer

Black-bellied Plover

Plate 53. LARGE AND MEDIUM GULLS

MEW GULL — 17″

Dark gray back and wings; *all-yellow, unmarked* bill; greenish-yellow legs. **Habitat:** Coasts, beaches, bays, flats. **Range:** Pacific Coast from British Columbia to Mexican border; winters throughout, but breeds only in Canadian portion.

HEERMANN'S GULL — 19″

White head and neck, in contrast with slate-gray body; lighter below; *red* bill; *blackish* legs. **Habitat:** Rocky coasts, islands, beaches, bays, inlets, estuaries. **Range:** Breeds south of Mexican border (Baja California); ranges *after* breeding season *north* to c. California; in nonbreeding season, wanders to Puget Sound, Washington, Vancouver Island.

RING-BILLED GULL — 19″

Pale gray back and wings; yellow bill with *black band;* yellow legs. **Habitat:** Lakes, rivers, beaches, bays, flooded and plowed fields; airports; golf courses, large lawns; refuse dumps, even municipal parking lots for food scraps! **Range:** S. Canada to Mexican border, inland south and east to Great Basin, Dakotas; winters north to s. British Columbia, s.e. Nevada, s.w. Utah, w. and s. Arizona, s.w. New Mexico, s. Texas, northeast to e. Kansas.

CALIFORNIA GULL — 21″

Pale gray back and wings; yellow bill with red and black spots; greenish-yellow legs. **Habitat:** Ocean beaches, lakes, rivers, marshes; farms; cities, piers. **Range:** S. Canada along Pacific Coast to Mexican border, inland to Great Basin, east to Dakotas; winters along coast to s. British Columbia, inland to s.e. California, s.w. Arizona.

HERRING GULL — 24″

Pale gray back and wings; yellow bill with red spot; pinkish legs. **Habitat:** Ocean beaches, lakes, rivers, harbors, fish piers, flooded fields; golf courses; refuse dumps. **Range:** Local in west, breeds in Arctic Canada; migrates throughout; winters from s. British Columbia to Mexican border, inland east to Idaho, much of California; also e. parts of Texas, Oklahoma, Kansas.

WESTERN GULL — 25″

Dark gray back and wings; yellow bill with red spot; pinkish legs. **Habitat:** Rocky cliffs, islets; sand beaches, mud flats, bays, estuaries. **Range:** Resident on Pacific Coast from s. British Columbia to Mexican border.

GLAUCOUS-WINGED GULL — 25″

Pale gray back and wings *(including wing tips);* yellow bill with red spot; pinkish legs. **Habitat:** Ocean beaches, bays, piers, dumps. **Range:** Breeds on Pacific Coast from s.w. British Columbia to n.w. Oregon; winters from s. British Columbia to Mexican border.

Plate 53. **LARGE AND MEDIUM GULLS**

Mew Gull

Heermann's Gull

Ring-
billed
Gull

California Gull

imm.
in flight

Herring
Gull

ad.

Western
Gull

Glaucous-winged
Gull

115

Plate 54. SMALL GULLS, TERNS

FRANKLIN'S GULL — 14″
Breeding—black hood; dark gray back and wings; *red* bill; dark red legs; wing tips black with white fore and aft, most evident in flight; nonbreeding—same, except head mainly whitish with dark patch behind eye, extending onto nape. **Habitat:** Inland prairies, marshes, lakes, sloughs. **Range:** Restricted mainly to w.c. North America, breeding from s. Alberta, Saskatchewan, Manitoba to s.e. Oregon, Idaho, n.w. Utah, n.w. Wyoming, Dakotas; migrates mainly through interior states, i.e., Great Basin, Rockies, w. plains; winters chiefly in w. South America.

BONAPARTE'S GULL — 13″
Light gray back and wings; *black* bill; bright red legs; wing tips with white wedge, noticeable in flight; breeding—black hood; nonbreeding—same, except white head with dark spot behind eye. **Habitat:** Ocean, bays, lakes, rivers. **Range:** Breeds from s. Canada northward; migrates throughout; winters—Pacific Coast north to Washington, s.w. Arizona to Gulf Coast.

LEAST TERN — 9″
Breeding—yellow bill with black tip; yellow legs; black cap with white forehead; nonbreeding—black bill; mainly white cap. **Habitat:** Ocean beaches, inlets, bays; sand bars in large rivers. **Range:** Breeds along Pacific Coast from c. California to Mexican border, lower Gulf Coast of s. Texas; inland on larger rivers (Colorado, Red, Missouri, Mississippi); winters mainly in tropics.

FORSTER'S TERN — 14″
Breeding—orange-red bill with black tip; black cap; nonbreeding—black bill; white head with black patch through eye. **Habitat:** Marshes, lakes, rivers, coasts. **Range:** Breeds inland and on coast from s. Canada to s. California, Nevada, Utah, Colorado, c. Kansas; migrates throughout; winters north to c. California, s. Arizona, s. Texas.

BLACK TERN — 9½″
Breeding—black bill and body; gray wings and tail; nonbreeding—similar, but with pied head, white below. **Habitat:** Inland marshes, lakes, ponds, sluggish rivers; fall migration—sea coasts, ocean. **Range:** Breeds inland from s. Canada to c. California, Nevada, Utah, Colorado, Kansas; migrates throughout; winters in tropics.

CASPIAN TERN — 21″
Our largest tern; *red* bill; slightly forked tail. **Habitat:** Lakes, rivers, beaches, bays, coastal flats, lagoons. **Range:** Breeds from Washington to Mexican border, from s. Canada to Nevada, Utah, Wyoming, Dakotas; lower Gulf Coast of Texas; winters north to s. California, Arizona, s. Texas.

ELEGANT TERN — 17″
Similar to Royal Tern, but smaller, with more slender bill—see Eastern Guide. **Habitat:** Sandy beaches; bays, estuaries. **Range:** Breeds on Pacific Coast of Mexico north to s. California; wanders north to central portions.

116

Plate 54. SMALL GULLS, TERNS

Franklin's Gull

summer

winter

summer

winter

Bonaparte's Gull

Least Tern

winter

Black Tern

Forster's Tern

winter

summer

summer

Caspian Tern

Elegant Tern

II. Further Comments on Plates

Plates 1 and 2 — **Reddish Birds, Reddish/Orange Birds**
With the exception of the two orange orioles, all of the others are bright red or have some amounts of red in their plumage. Of the eight species which are finch-like, all have heavy bills for cracking seeds. The two tanagers and both orioles are mainly fruit- and insect-eaters. The one flycatcher, as its name suggests, feeds entirely on insects, but is placed here because of its bright red color. The closely related Cardinal and Pyrrhuloxia have *crests*.

Plate 3 — **Yellowish Birds**
All of the birds on this plate either are mostly yellow or have some yellow in their plumage. These birds are solidly colored, with conspicuous bars or patches on their wings, with the exception of the heavily streaked Pine Siskin. The six finch-like birds are related to the oriole and the tanager.

Plates 4 and 5 — **Warblers**
A large family of active and mostly brightly colored small birds with slender bills. The one notable exception, the Yellow-breasted Chat, is much larger. The warblers are misnamed, since many of them do not warble at all, but instead have buzzy, insect-like notes. Others, such as the Common Yellowthroat, have more distinctive and/or attractive songs.

As with most of the other birds in this volume, the plates show the warblers in their readily identifiable plumages, i.e., spring and summer males in bright breeding dress. Many, but not all, warblers have some yellow in them, and in these two plates, fourteen out of seventeen species do.

Six warblers on these plates are wide-ranging, occurring from coast to coast, and are therefore shown in both the Eastern and Western Guides, namely: the Yellow, Wilson's, Nashville, and Yellow-rumped ("Audubon's") warblers; also the Common Yellowthroat and the American Redstart. Ten other species are entirely or basically western in distribution, as may be seen in the text opposite the color plates.

Nearly all of these warblers possess one or two distinctive field marks that readily separate them from one another. For example, the Common Yellowthroat has a conspicuous black mask. Two other species are instantly recognized by bright red areas—the Painted Redstart and the Red-faced Warbler.

The following important questions about field marks should be answered in identifying warblers:

1. Do they have either wing bars or wing patches, or do they lack these marks?

2. Are they streaked below, or are they without streaks?

3. Are they yellow or mainly yellow below?

4. Are they white or mainly white below?

5. Do they have conspicuous black markings anywhere about the head, body, or tail?

Plate 6 — **Greenish/Grayish Birds**

The two birds at the top of this plate are nearly as small as hummingbirds and are known as kinglets. They are related to the Old World warblers and are extremely active and restless—flitting about continuously. Both kinglets have prominent head markings, the Ruby-crowned with an eye *ring,* the Golden-crowned with an eye *stripe.*

The four vireos are relatively sluggish, thick-billed birds, quite unlike the active, restless, and slender-billed warblers, which they superficially resemble. Both the Gray and the Solitary have wing bars and eye *rings,* whereas the Red-eyed and the Warbling *lack* wing bars and possess eye stripes. Incidentally, all birds on this plate range from coast to coast, except the Gray Vireo, which is strictly southwestern.

Plate 7 — **Flycatchers**

Flycatchers' behavior is unique. They fly out from a perch for an insect and almost invariably return to the same perch. The upright stance of these birds is also a good means of identification.

Some things to remember. Of the eight flycatcher species on this plate, both the Western Kingbird and the Ash-throated Flycatcher have a gray throat and chest with yellow breast and belly; the Black Phoebe and the Eastern Kingbird are black and white; Say's Phoebe has a cinnamon belly; the Western Flycatcher has an olive breast and a yellowish belly; finally, both the Olive-sided Flycatcher and the Western Wood Pewee are drab and somber. Check color plate with text opposite for details.

Plates 8 and 9 — **Grayish Birds**

As the two plates indicate, these birds either are predominantly gray or have a certain amount of gray in their plumage. The species shown on Plate 8 are much larger than those on Plate 9. The flycatcher may be easily identified by its long, scissor-like tail. The short-tailed Dipper is always found actively flitting about mountain streams, either on the rocks or in the water. Superficially, it looks like a large, overgrown wren.

The jay, nutcracker, and solitaire are confined mostly to mountains or in the North, whereas the shrike, mockingbird, and flycatcher are mainly southern in range.

The small birds on Plate 9 consist of two families: the uppermost are gnatcatchers with longish tails; the others are titmice, two of which are crested. The three chickadees lack crests, as do the Verdin (Yellow-headed Tit) and the Bushtit. Most of these birds are very tame and can be studied at close range.

Plate 10 — **Bluish Birds**
The five birds on this plate represent two different families: the jays and the Belted Kingfisher, totally unrelated. The latter, as its name suggests, feeds exclusively on fish. The jays are omnivorous, eating nuts, seeds, fruit, suet, and even bird eggs on occasion.

Three of these five birds are similar in that they possess crests, the two middle jays having pointed ones, the kingfisher a bushy-shaped crest. The remaining two species—the Scrub Jay and the Pinyon Jay—are uncrested. The Blue Jay and the Steller's Jay are in the same genus.

Plate 11 — **Bluish/Reddish Birds**
The seven birds on this plate are among the brightest species anywhere in this field guide. The Painted Bunting, especially, might be described as gaudy, and the Lazuli Bunting and both bluebirds are not far behind; and yet, the Blue Grosbeak and both Indigo and Varied buntings—bright as they are in full sunlight—look black at a distance or in poor light.

The upper five species are finches, with heavy bills adapted for husking hard-shelled nuts and sunflower seeds. The two bluebirds are members of the thrush family and have slender bills suitable for soft-bodied insects and fruits.

Plates 12 to 14 — **Sparrows**
The birds on these three plates may be grouped into two main categories:
1. the mostly grayish sparrows on Plate 12, and the generally brownish sparrows on Plates 13 and 14
2. whether they are streaked or unstreaked, as follows: completely streaked above and below: the Fox, Song, Savannah, and Vesper sparrows; completely unstreaked above and below: the three juncos and the Black-throated Sparrow on Plate 12.

All of the remaining sparrows are either unstreaked below or, in the case of Harris' and Sage, partially streaked. Study these birds carefully according to these categories and then progress to each species for its outstanding field marks, given on the text pages opposite the color plates.

Plates 15 to 17 — **Brownish Birds**
The six wrens on Plate 15 are small to medium-sized and noted for their active and restless habits, as well as for the frequent cocking-up of their tails. The unrelated but somewhat similar-looking Wrentit of the West Coast also cocks its tail, but is more secretive than the wrens, often hiding in scrub and bushes.

The wrens are confined mainly to special habitats. The familiar House Wren is found near buildings, Bewick's Wren in thickets and hedgerows, the Marsh Wren—as its name implies—in cattail marshes and wet reedy places. The three western species—as *their* names specify—occur in much drier areas, among rocks and in canyons. Finally, the largest of the wrens is found mainly in cactus deserts. It should be stated that all but the Marsh Wrens frequent feeders on occasion.

The eight birds on Plate 16 belong to two different families. The

120

towhees are mainly ground-dwelling, sparrow-like birds that feed chiefly on seeds. The four thrashers inhabit brush and thickets, and superficially resemble thrushes. As can be seen by their slender and somewhat decurved bills, their diet is more varied—berries, insects, and some seeds. All eight species may be found in arid regions, although both the Rufous-sided ("Spotted") Towhee and the California Thrasher dwell in towns and gardens as well.

The five thrushes and two unrelated waxwings on Plate 17 have one thing in common—they all feed on fruit and insects. The very familiar and versatile American Robin is, of course, best known for its preference for lawns and golf courses and for its consumption of earthworms. Unlike this well-known and conspicuous bird, the beautiful Varied Thrush is much more retiring and lives mostly in humid forests; in bad winter weather, however, it may be observed at feeders. The three brown-backed thrushes are also relatively shy, but are often found in the open if the observer is quiet and cautious.

The two waxwings often occur in large flocks, especially in winter, when they may be readily observed in berry-bearing trees and bushes. They are at times extraordinarily tame and can be approached at close range. In the warmer months, when they pair off and feed extensively on insects, they may be watched at leisure flycatching near wooded ponds and streams. Waxwings are sleek and handsome and are the only birds on these three plates that are crested.

Plate 18 — **Grassland Birds**
The seven birds on this plate, belonging to four different families, comprise a miscellaneous assortment of predominantly brownish birds living in open grasslands. The largest bird—the Western Meadowlark—has a short tail, and a black **V** or chevron across its bright yellow breast. The smaller, similar-looking Horned Lark and Dickcissel are unrelated, as are the tail-wagging Water Pipit and the distinctive winter bird, the Snow Bunting. Finally, the two longspurs are found in grasslands, the Lapland being a winter visitor from the high Arctic tundra.

Plates 19 and 20 — **Blackish Birds**
Five different families are represented on these two plates. The crested Phainopepla is a member of the waxwing group; the Lark Bunting is a finch; the introduced Starling is an Old World bird; the Black-billed Magpie, the American Crow, and the Northern Raven belong to the family Corvidae; the Bobolink, the two cowbirds, the three blackbirds, and both grackles are all members of the family Icteridae.

Although many of the above are entirely black or blackish with iridescent plumage, a few have other colors, such as the Yellow-headed Blackbird, the Bobolink with buff and white in breeding plumage, and the Black-billed Magpie with much white.

Many of these birds inhabit open country, such as marshes, grasslands, and even deserts, while the Northern Raven lives in forested regions, as well as open, arid areas. The ubiquitous American Crow is found everywhere.

Plate 21 — **Tree Clingers**

The birds on this plate have one thing in common—they spend much of their time on trees. The Brown Creeper and the four woodpeckers forage on the tree trunks and branches by climbing *up*. The three nuthatches, on the other hand, descend head *down*.

The larger White-breasted Nuthatch feeds chiefly on the trunks and larger branches of deciduous hardwoods, while the two smaller species are found in conifers, mainly among the smaller branches and even probing the cones at the tips of the evergreens.

The Brown Creeper is almost always observed spiraling up a tree, its dull brown back blending in with the bark; its decurved bill is distinctive.

The four woodpeckers on this plate and the twelve species on Plates 22 and 23 are discussed in detail below.

Plates 22 and 23 — **Woodpeckers**

Including the four species on Plate 21, there are sixteen woodpeckers in all, ranging in size from the spectacular crow-sized, crested Pileated Woodpecker to the very small Downy Woodpecker.

These birds are most frequently seen in an upright position on the trunk of a tree or even on a utility pole. With their chisel-shaped bills and stiffly pointed tails, they climb in search of boring insects. The exception is the familiar Northern Flicker, which often feeds on the ground in pursuit of ants.

Most woodpeckers have black and white patterns of some sort, either in patches or in stripes and bars, or spots. They usually have some red on the head. Only the Red-headed Woodpecker, however, has the head entirely red, as does the male Red-breasted Sapsucker.

The familiar Downy Woodpecker and the less numerous Hairy Woodpecker are replicas of each other, the latter being the larger of the two species.

Most unusual, perhaps, is the great difference between the sexes of the Williamson's Sapsucker. The male is solid black and white with a red throat and yellow belly, whereas the female has a brown head and a zebra-patterned back, tail, and sides. The female was once even described as a different species until, many years later, it was found breeding with the male.

Plate 24 — **Swallows**

These graceful aerialists are adept at catching flying insects on the wing and are most often seen in flight. Nevertheless, they may also be observed perched on overhead wires in long rows, and at times they can be approached at fairly close range. At these roadside gatherings, as many as seven species may be observed on rare occasions. Their differences in size, shape, pattern, and color will be readily noticed.

The Purple Martin, our largest swallow, is the only species in this family in our area that is represented by different-looking sexes. The male is uniformly dark and glossy blue-black; the female is dark above, pale gray below.

Most of our swallows have tails that are either slightly forked or notched. The closely related Barn and Cliff swallows, however, have tails of vastly different shape: the former's is deeply forked, while the latter's is square-shaped.

These characteristics are of great importance in separating the different species, either in flight or at rest.

Plate 25 — Swifts, Nightjars

All three swifts and one of the two nightjars included on this plate are strictly western species. The members of these two families are exclusively aerial insect feeders, and the observer rarely sees them except when they are in flight.

Swifts live up to their name, being among the fastest-flying of all birds. Only the White-throated Swift is bicolored, having a conspicuous black and white pattern.

Of the two nightjars, the familiar Common Nighthawk may be easily recognized by the prominent white bands on its long, pointed wings. The smaller Poorwill, on the other hand, has no white markings on its short, rounded wings. Moreover, it is seen much less frequently than the Common Nighthawk.

Plate 26 — Hummingbirds

Often called "winged jewels," these smallest of all birds are well represented in the West. No fewer than eight of more than sixteen species are depicted here. All occur north of Mexico, the majority being found in southern Arizona, mostly during the summer months.

Only males are shown on the color plate, with the exception of the Black-chinned Hummingbird (both sexes illustrated). This species is the western representative of the familiar Ruby-throated Hummingbird, the only member of the family found in the East. Whereas the drab females look much alike, the glittering males may be told apart by carefully noting the gorget (throat) color and head marking. This is best done when these birds are either perched on a twig or feeding among the flowers.

Plate 27 — Cuckoo, Pigeons

The one cuckoo on this plate ranges widely. Seven species of pigeons and doves are represented. The distinction between pigeons and doves is one of size only, the former being larger, the latter generally smaller; but there is some overlap. The largest is the Band-tailed Pigeon at about 15 inches; the smallest is the sparrow-sized Ground Dove at about 6½″ inches.

The most widespread of this group is the familiar and numerous Mourning Dove. The most restricted is the introduced Spotted Dove (from Asia), now well established in southern California. Introduced from Europe, the semidomesticated Rock (Domestic) Pigeon is well known to urban and suburban dwellers.

Plates 28 and 29 — Gamebirds

These birds are all chicken-like, with the Bobwhite the smallest, the Wild Turkey the largest.

Unlike the Eastern Guide, which has only one plate and four species, the Western Guide has two plates and fourteen species. Moreover, all four eastern gamebirds are repeated in the current volume, plus *ten* all-western gamebirds. The two plates are divided into the smaller gamebirds and the larger ones. The first plate consists of five quails (the Bobwhite is a quail) and two partridges—both introduced from Eurasia. The second plate includes the Wild Turkey, the Ring-necked Pheasant—introduced from western Asia—and four kinds of grouse.

The last species is included here with the gamebirds, as it has the appearance of being chicken-like. However, it is actually a large ground cuckoo—the well-known and conspicuous Roadrunner of the southwestern deserts.

Plates 30 to 33 — **Hawks**
No fewer than nineteen species of hawk-like birds or diurnal raptors appear on these four plates. They consist of two vultures, two eagles, five buteos, two accipiters, one each of Osprey and Northern Harrier (Marsh Hawk), two kites, and four falcons.

Many of these species occur from coast to coast or nearly so. The Swainson's and Ferruginous hawks, as well as the Prairie Falcon, are exclusively western in distribution. The Golden Eagle is quite common in the West, but rare and local in the East. The Black Vulture and Mississippi Kite, however, are mostly southeastern in range, while the Red-shouldered Hawk is mainly an eastern species, with an isolated population in California. Finally, the Black-shouldered Kite is restricted to the Pacific coastal areas of Oregon and California; also the Gulf Coast of Texas.

The most important clue in hawk identification is the shape of the wings and tail, especially noticeable in overhead flight; distinctive also is the manner of flight. The plates and accompanying text emphasize patterns and colors, especially when these birds are perched, sometimes at close range. Only adults are illustrated, unless otherwise noted.

Plates 34 and 35 — **Owls**
The ten species of owls on these two plates range from the Great Horned Owl, as large as a Red-tailed Hawk—both nearly 2 feet in length—to the world's smallest owl, the tiny Elf Owl, as small as a House Sparrow (6 inches).

Only two of the ten species have dark eyes—the Barn Owl and the Spotted Owl—imparting a "mild" appearance; the remaining species have light-colored, yellowish eyes, which give them a somewhat "fierce" expression.

Three owls possess head tufts—the Great Horned, Long-eared, and Western Screech owls. Their head tufts are strictly ornamental and have nothing to do with hearing. The other seven species are tuftless, although the Short-eared Owl, as its name implies, has tiny head tufts, not visible in the field.

With the exception of the Burrowing and Short-eared owls, both open-country and ground-dwelling species, the others inhabit tree groves to dense forests. The Barn and Great Horned owls, however, sometimes nest on cliffs or among rocks.

All owls have large heads and appear to be without a neck.

Plate 36 — **Geese, Swans**

There are many white birds, but in our part of the world, few are as large as a swan. Swans are much larger than geese and have longer necks. When they are in flight, they look enormous with head and outstretched neck as long as the body!

Both species of swans have twice the bulk of Snow Geese. In addition to being completely white, including their wing tips, the two western swans have *black* bills, whereas Snow Geese possess conspicuous black wing tips and have *pink* bills.

The biggest problem for beginners lies in distinguishing geese from ducks. As a rule, geese have longer necks than ducks (just as swans differ from geese). They are generally larger, and their bodies are heavier. The Brant (a goose) is the exception: it is Mallard-sized.

Finally, geese are frequently seen grazing on land, particularly in fields and on golf courses. Ducks and swans are more partial to water—most often observed swimming.

Plates 37 to 41 — **Ducks**

For many birders, ducks are difficult to identify in flight, except after long experience. For this reason, the illustrations show them only on water or on land, where one has the best opportunity to identify them.

As you go through the plates, you will notice that ducks are grouped as follows:

Plates 37 and 38—Tipping Ducks. These ducks feed mostly in shallow water by tipping and upending on or near the surface of the water; they also forage on land.

Plates 39 to 41—Diving Ducks. These ducks chiefly inhabit deep water, where they feed by diving from the surface; they obtain much of their food at or near the bottom.

As for color differences, ducks may also be grouped according to whether their heads are all or mostly green; for example, the Mallard, the Shoveler, and both the common and the red-breasted mergansers all have green heads. Within this group there are also marked differences. The Mallard has a white ring around its neck, the Shoveler has a spoon-shaped bill, one of the two mergansers is crested, and both have long red bills.

One might also categorize ducks by various conspicuous white patches on the head, wings, or body. Many have prominent white markings—Pintail, the American Wigeon (Baldpate), the Shoveler, the Blue-winged Teal, the Ruddy Duck, the Black-bellied Whistling Duck, the Canvasback, the Surf Scoter, the two goldeneyes, the Bufflehead, and all three mergansers.

Finally, the tipping ducks are found chiefly on sheltered ponds, marshes, and wooded swamps, whereas the deep-water diving ducks frequent large lakes and reservoirs, coastal bays and estuaries, as well as the ocean itself, albeit close to shore.

Plate 42 — Alcids, Loons

Loons are black and white goose-sized divers with short, thick necks and sharp, pointed bills. On the water, loons can be distinguished from cormorants by the position of their bills—bills of loons pointing straight ahead, those of cormorants slanting upward.

Both the guillemot and the murre are members of the alcid family—black and white duck-like seabirds, but with pointed bills. This primarily far-northern family includes auks, murres, guillemots, and puffins, among others. When nesting, they inhabit rocky shores and cliffs.

Plate 43 — Grebes

Grebes, loon-like with lobed feet, sit low in the water, appear to be tailless, and have dagger-like bills. They are therefore easily distinguished from ducks. The small Pied-billed Grebe, however, has a thick, chicken-like bill. The very large Western Grebe may be told easily by its long, gleaming white neck, which is swan-like.

All Grebes, when diving from the surface, sink into the water and reappear at another spot.

Plate 44 — Rails, Gallinule, Coot

The American Coot and the Common Gallinule (Moorhen) are duck-like birds with chicken-like bills. The white bill contrasting with the dark gray body is a sure sign of the American Coot, while the red, yellow-tipped bill is a field mark of the Common Gallinule, or Moorhen.

The two long-billed rails are rather chicken-like in shape and the diminutive Sora has a short, stubby bill. All have one thing in common—they skulk in dense reed beds of both salt- and freshwater marshes and are usually difficult to see well.

Plate 45 — Cormorants, Pelicans

The three species of cormorants in our area are large black goose-like birds in flight, but more loon-like when on the water, and like loons, they dive from the surface of the water. Cormorants have hooked bills, but this feature is observed only at close range. When perched, they stand erect—often with their wings stretched out to dry. Unlike nearly all the other birds, cormorants do not possess waterproof feathers, since they lack oil glands. During migration, cormorants are frequently seen flying overhead with steady wingbeats in very large numbers, either in long lines or in V-shaped flocks. Unlike geese, however, they are silent.

The pelicans, of which there are two kinds in our area, are familiar to all. One—the White Pelican—is mainly an inhabitant of inland fresh waters, although it spends the winter months along the Gulf coast of Texas. The other—the Brown Pelican—lives near the ocean along the beaches. Lines of these prehistoric-looking birds alternately flap and glide in unison low over the surf. They plunge from moderate heights into the sea for fish, and often perch on posts, piers, and even fishing boats. Unlike the Brown Pelican, the huge White Pelican fishes from the surface in shallow waters. In flight, these spectacular birds with gleaming white plumage and partially

126

jet-black wings also alternately flap and sail in unison, sometimes in large flocks.

Plates 46 and 47 — Long-legged Waders

Herons are wading birds whose habitat is often the best clue to their identification. They can usually be seen picking their way slowly through shallow water in marshes (the two bitterns) or along mudflats searching for fish, frogs, and other aquatic forms of life. They may also be observed roosting together in large numbers in trees and bushes near water where they breed. They may have either long or short legs and long or short necks, but they all have long bills, except for the field-inhabiting, insect-eating Cattle Egret and the seminocturnal Black-crowned Night Heron.

The various white forms known as egrets, of which there are three species in our area, are members of this family (Great, Snowy, and Cattle egrets). People often confuse egrets and herons. All egrets are herons, but the reverse is not true—all herons are *not* egrets.

As for the Cattle Egret, this immigrant from Africa has spread far and wide and has become established over much of the United States, although it is somewhat local in the West. Cattle Egrets feed on various insects that are flushed from the grass by moving cattle, other livestock, and even farm tractors.

Unlike other herons, the American Bittern is solitary and reluctant to fly. For safety it relies on its cryptic pattern and coloration; as it stands motionless, its streaked breast blends in with the reeds. Although often skulking in marsh grass, chiefly cattails but also the giant reed (*Phragmites*), the diminutive Least Bittern may be seen in short flights, skimming just above the top of the marsh, or more rarely observed grasping cattail stems and even climbing among them.

Many people mistakenly call herons cranes. Cranes differ from the superficially similar but unrelated herons, particularly when in flight. Unlike herons, cranes fly with necks outstretched and in a V-formation, or in long lines, like geese; they also flap and glide. Herons, on the other hand, fly with necks kinked or folded in, and with slow, steady wingbeats in loose flocks. The common crane in our area is the gray-colored Sandhill Crane.

As for the White-faced Ibis, the slender, decurved bill of this bird separates it immediately from all the other straight-billed species on these two plates.

Plates 48 to 52 — Shorebirds

The shorebirds—or "waders," as they are sometimes called—frequent the shores of lakes and rivers and the edges of marshes, as well as tidal flats and even ocean beaches. They reflect a diversity of types which is matched by their many different names. There are two major subdivisions, based primarily on bill shapes that are adaptations for feeding: (1) the plovers, with short, stubby bills and (2) the sandpipers and allies, with long, slender bills. In addition, the following names are used in this very large and diversified group: "oystercatcher," "stilt," "avocet," "godwit," "curlew," "whim-brel," "Willet," "yellowlegs," "dowitcher," "knot," "turnstone," "snipe,"

"Dunlin," and "phalarope," plus two strictly Pacific Coast shorebirds—"Surfbird" and "tattler."

One of the first things to look for in shorebirds is the length and shape of their bills. For example, oystercatchers have laterally compressed, knife-like bills for opening and extracting shellfish; avocets and godwits have upturned bills; curlews and whimbrels have downturned ones; dowitchers and snipes have long, straight, slender bills for probing deep into the mud and ooze; stilts, Willets, yellowlegs, and many sandpipers have long, needle-like bills for feeding in deep water and for picking up aquatic insects and marine forms; finally, plovers have shorter bills for picking up snails and other small types of animal life directly from the ground or from shallow pools, mudflats, and sand beaches.

Plates 53 and 54 — **Gulls, Terns**

The most numerous and familiar whitish or grayish birds seen perched or flying at the seashore or near lakes and other bodies of water are the gulls, which scavenge scraps from refuse dumps and even parking lots! Several features distinguish gulls from their relatives, the terns. Gulls are usually, but not always, larger than terns. Gull bills are mostly heavier, and slightly hooked at the tip, whereas those of terns are pointed. Gulls keep their bills pointed straight ahead when in flight, while terns keep theirs pointed downward. Gulls pick up their food on land or from the surface of the water, and they never dive. Terns dive headfirst into the water for fish.

Terns generally are more graceful-looking, especially on the wing. Many species have forked tails and distinctive black caps, the larger species with slight crests. Several of the smaller gulls have black hoods in spring and summer, but the medium-sized and larger gulls are white-headed the year round. Young gulls are mottled with gray; they are uniformly brownish when very young. A glance at these two plates will enable the reader to distinguish between the groups.

III. Attracting Birds

As the sport and hobby of birding have grown over the years, so too have bird feeders, which not only bring more species to the backyard but also help the birds themselves, especially in colder areas where snow and ice may cover up their food. In retrospect, it can be seen that feeders have been an important factor in the rapid spread of some species (for example, the Cardinal) to areas where they had been rare or even unknown. As conservation has become of widespread interest to millions, so too has increased awareness of the need to protect and aid birds. As a result, setting out feeders and gardening with an eye to attracting birds have become national pastimes. It is obvious that the greater the variety of birds, the greater the enjoyment of backyard birding.

Getting actively involved in feeding birds requires selecting feeders, setting them up in the right location, and filling them with a good mixture of food.

Feeders may be purchased in hardware stores, garden centers, nurseries, pet shops, and supermarkets. They range from simple feeders to elaborate bird "cafeterias." They can even be built by the unhandiest birder. In selecting a feeder, remember that all you want is something to hold the food; it does not have to be complicated. Avoid metal feeders, since they heat up in the summer sun and become tacky in freezing weather.

Feeders can be easily fashioned out of common objects around the house. A plastic bleach bottle, for example, can be converted into a feeder, as can milk cartons, shoe boxes, and small wooden crates. Containers in which doors and windows have been cut can be suspended from a tree with metal coat hangers. A flat board with a raised edge around it to keep the seeds from spilling over also makes an efficient feeder. A shallow candy box on the bedroom windowsill can serve as an alarm clock, since chirping birds are quite regular—and noisy—clamoring for food early in the morning.

Store-bought feeders come in all sizes, shapes, and materials. Some are made of redwood, and have glass sides and a shelf for food. Others look like plastic bubbles, and can be hung up almost anywhere. There are also seed silos, post feeders, hummingbird feeders, and even small transparent boxes that can be attached to the windowpane with a suction cup. Many feeders dole out the seeds a little at a time, avoiding spillage and protecting the food from inclement weather.

Up to now, we have been talking about feeders used primarily for seed. Feeders are not confined to seed eaters, however. Many also have suet racks for insect-eating birds, especially woodpeckers and nuthatches. Metal racks may even be nailed directly onto the tree trunk. Mesh bags (the kind that hold onions and oranges) may be filled with chunks of suet and suspended from a hook or branch; be sure that they swing freely, otherwise aggressive Starlings, which don't like the motion, will take over. The suet and fat should be discontinued in warm weather, since they melt or become rancid.

As for hummingbirds, if you have a garden, watch such flowers as trumpetvine, petunias, salvia, or jewelweed. Hummers are especially attracted to red and orange colors. A hummingbird feeder filled with sugar-water and a little red tape or paint on the bottle is another way to lure these birds into your yard.

Before putting a feeder into operation, be sure that its location is right. The ideal place is out of the wind, near natural cover, in an area that is sunny in winter and shady in summer. A kitchen window is frequently the perfect place. The ability to see the feeder from the house is the first prerequisite. Next, you want to see *birds* in it, and not squirrels. The feeder should be set up where squirrels cannot decimate the food supply and where cats cannot decimate the bird supply. Squirrels are very acrobatic. Consequently, baffles above and below feeders are necessary to keep them out, and the feeders must be away from trees and bushes so that the squirrels cannot leap into them. Once the station is working, food should not be placed on the ground, where a preoccupied bird can become easy prey of a cat. This is not to say that birds, on their own, won't feed on the ground; many do, but at least you won't be responsible for any mishap that might occur. To keep Rock Pigeons away, enclosures can be made with wire mesh large enough for small birds but too small for Rock Pigeons.

Now that the feeder is ready, what kind of seed should you get? Many commercial mixes of wild bird feed include large amounts of milo (round red seeds) or buckwheat, oats, and wheat, all of which you will find left behind in the feeder. Your best bet is sunflower seed, the favorite of Cardinals, grosbeaks, chickadees, titmice, finches, and jays. For smaller seed-eating birds, white and red millet, as well as cracked corn, is popular. While a number of birds favor peanut hearts, this feed is also very attractive to Starlings, which can quickly become pests. If you would like to try for goldfinches, Pine Siskins, and Purple Finches, thistle seed (also called niger seed) is sure to do the trick.

Many table scraps are also good for enticing birds, as are stale dry cereals, doughnuts, crackers and bread (especially favored by blackbirds), and fruit—grapes, cherries, apples, oranges, and bananas for Mockingbirds and orioles. Near the shore and at ponds, bread will be gobbled up by gulls and ducks.

After choosing a feeder (or more than one, to attract a larger variety of birds), you must decide when to start using it. Winter time in the colder areas is the essential period for feeding birds; do not stop until mild weather sets in.

It takes time to establish a feeder. You have to be patient and wait for birds to discover it. Unless birds are hard-pressed for food, they are as likely to go beetle-grubbing or seed-gathering in an empty lot as to visit a feeder. Bad weather and a shortage of food, however, will bring them to you, by having an easily available supply of their favorite foods. The variety of birds that come to feeders will depend on the variety of food put out. In warmer regions, the feeding station is more fun for the birder than a necessity for the birds. In colder areas, you must keep in mind that once a feeding station has been established in the fall, many birds become dependent on it. So don't start a feeding program if you are going to be away in the midwinter months and will be leaving the feeder untended.

Once the feeding routine has become established, birds will continue as steady customers until spring, when buds, berries, and bugs are plentiful. At this time, put out some yarn, cotton, and strips of paper for nest-building birds.

If feeding is prolonged into the summer, adult birds may bring their young to the feeder, and eventually the young will come by themselves. Remember that young birds are unwary and easily caught by cats. If you continue to feed birds, you must make sure that cats don't come for a free meal too. To keep them from pouncing out of the shrubs, a low metal or chicken-wire fence should be installed at the edge of flower borders, particularly thick borders (lily and iris beds), which are favorite hideouts for cats.

Water is as much a part of a feeding station as food. Winter and summer, birds need drinking water. Some birds will also bathe, even on bitterly cold days. Heating mechanisms may be installed in bird baths to keep them from freezing. In summer, on hot dry days, an oscillating lawn sprinkler will bring birds down from the treetops—small birds like warblers and kinglets that you never suspected were around. An old leaking bucket filled with water and dripping into a pan will serve the same purpose.

Landscaping for food and shelter is a necessity for a successful feeding station. Geographic location and local climate will influence the selection of plants. Once started, planting of shrubs and trees may seem an overwhelming task, but nature will help if given a chance. Frequently, seedlings will pop up among bushes from a stray seed or from bird droppings.

Deciduous and evergreen shrubs, trees, and vines should be planted for their buds, fruits, or seeds—and are listed at the end of this chapter. Many deciduous trees are easily planted, and in early spring they produce buds and flowers, as well as foliage, that attract insect-eating birds. Alders, birches, and poplars also produce catkins, which provide seeds for later consumption. Cherry trees can be transplanted from the wild or might just appear from a stray seed dropped by a bird.

Aside from organized gardening, there are a number of miscellaneous suggestions that might be helpful. Thick, unrestrained shrubbery will provide good cover, as well as nesting and roosting sites. A discarded Christmas tree set up in the yard makes a good windbreak and shelter for birds. A wild corner given over to bittersweet, catbrier, chokeberry, honeysuckle, pokeberry, and Virginia creeper will become an impenetrable tangle appealing to nesting Northern Mockingbirds and other thicket-haunting birds. Incidentally, dead trees or limbs should be left for woodpeckers. If a utility wire runs through your property, watch it for perching flycatchers or migrating swallows. A well-trimmed lawn attracts American Robins and ant-pursuing Northern Flickers. The base of a privet hedge adjacent to an open lawn may be preferred by thrushes, sparrows, and buntings.

In addition to creating a sanctuary for birds with feeders, bird baths, landscaping, and food, nest boxes can be provided for breeding birds. In bluebird country, for example, there is intense competition between other hole-nesting birds and shy native bluebirds, which give way to aggressive Starlings and House Sparrows. Entrance holes should be small enough for the bluebird alone. Tree Swallows might move into a bluebird house, but they are welcome guests. Just put out more houses, and there will be plenty of room for both. An open area without trees, not far from water, is a perfect site for a Purple Martin house. In return for the lodging, the birds will feast on mosquitoes and other noxious insects.

SHRUBS, TREES, AND VINES WITH THEIR BUDS, FRUITS, OR SEEDS

English Name	Scientific Name	English Name	Scientific Name
Alder	*Alnus*	Holly	*Ilex*
Ash	*Fraxinus*	Honeysuckle	*Lonicera*
Aspen	*Populus*	Huckleberry	*Vaccinium*
Barberry	*Berberis*	Manzanita	*Arctostaphylos*
Bayberry	*Myrica*	Maple	*Acer*
Beech	*Fagus*	Mountain Ash	*Sorbus*
Birch	*Betula*	Mulberry	*Morus*
Bittersweet	*Celastrus*	Oak	*Quercus*
Blackberry	*Rubus*	Pecan	*Carya*
Blueberry	*Vaccinium*	Persimmon	*Diospyros*
Box Elder	*Acer*	Pine	*Pinus*
Buckthorn	*Rhamnus*	Pokeberry	*Phytolacca*
Catbriar	*Smilax*	Poplar	*Populus*
Cherry	*Prunus*	Privet	*Ligustrum*
Chokeberry	*Aronia*	Raspberry	*Rubus*
Cottonwood	*Populus*	Red Cedar	*Juniperus*
Crabapple	*Malus*	Sassafras	*Sassafras*
Currant	*Ribes*	Shadbush	*Amelanchier*
Dogwood	*Cornus*	Sour Gum (Tupelo)	*Nyssa*
Elderberry	*Sambucus*	Spicebush	*Benzoin*
Fir	*Abies*	Spruce	*Picea*
Firethorn	*Pyracantha*	Sumac	*Rhus*
Grape (Wild)	*Vitis*	Sweet Gum	*Liquidambar*
Hackberry	*Celtis*	Viburnum	*Viburnum*
Hawthorn	*Crataegus*	Virginia Creeper	*Parthenocissus*
Hemlock	*Tsuga*	Walnut	*Juglans*
Hercules Club	*Aralia*	Yew	*Taxus*

HUMMINGBIRD FLOWERS

English Name	Scientific Name	English Name	Scientific Name
Acacia	*Acacia*	Jimsonweed	*Datura*
Aloe	*Aloe*	Lantana	*Lantana*
Barrel Cactus	*Echinocactus*	Larkspur	*Delphinium*
Beardtongue	*Penstemon*	Locust	*Robinia*
Beebalm	*Monarda*	Mesquite	*Prosopis*
Bergamot	*Monarda*	Morning Glory	*Ipomoea*
Cardinal Flower	*Lobelia*	Nasturtium	*Tropaeolum*
Century Plant	*Agave*	Ocotillo	*Fouquieria*
Cholla Cactus	*Opuntia*	Paloverde	*Cercidium*
Columbine	*Aquilegia*	Petunia	*Petunia*
Coral Bells	*Heuchera*	Phlox	*Phlox*
Creosote Bush	*Larrea*	Redbud	*Cercis*
Fuchsia	*Fuchsia*	Redhot Poker	*Kniphofia*
Geranium	*Geranium*	Saguaro Cactus	*Carnegiea*
Hibiscus	*Hibiscus*	Salvia	*Salvia*
Hollyhock	*Althaea*	Spanish Bayonet	*Yucca*
Indian Paintbrush	*Castileja*	Thistle	*Cirsium*
Jewelweed	*Impatiens*	Trumpetvine	*Bignonia*

BIRDS ATTRACTED TO FRUIT, INSECTS, NECTAR, SEEDS, SUET, AND WATER

English Family Name(s)	Scientific Family Name
Blackbirds, Orioles	Icteridae
Buntings, Finches, Sparrows	Fringillidae
Creepers	Certhiidae
Crows, Jays	Corvidae
Gnatcatchers, Kinglets	Sylviidae
Hummingbirds	Trochilidae
Mockingbirds, Thrashers	Mimidae
Nuthatches	Sittidae
Pigeons, Doves	Columbidae
Roadrunner (Cuckoos)	Cuculidae
Tanagers	Thraupidae
Thrushes	Turdidae
Titmice	Paridae
Warblers	Parulidae
Waxwings	Bombycillidae
Woodpeckers	Picidae
Wrens	Troglodytidae
Wrentit	Timaliidae

Appendixes

Optical Equipment

Whether at home or away, one can watch birds with the naked eye, but to identify them correctly and to study them well, some optical equipment is essential. At first, perhaps, 2- to 3-power opera glasses might suffice, but in order to bring a bird up close enough to observe fine details, a pair of prism binoculars is a must.

Start with a lightweight pair, the magnification of which should be no more than 7 to 8 power; that is, the bird under observation should be at least seven times closer than it is without binoculars. Those of either 7 $\times$ 35 or, even better, 7 $\times$ 50 are undoubtedly the best. Binoculars more powerful than 7 or 8 will usually be heavier and more cumbersome to use. Remember—the figure after the $\times$ represents the amount of light; 50 is better than 35.

Make certain that the binoculars you buy have a central focus, that is, a wheel or other device in the center to turn or focus both lenses quickly at the same time. This is most important, especially with moving birds, for which instant focusing is imperative.

When purchasing optical equipment, make sure that the lenses are clear and that no distortions are present. Do *not* buy binoculars until you have looked through them. They must be in perfect order in every respect, including proper alignment, so as not to strain your eyes. When the binoculars are not in use, keep them in their carrying case.

For those birds that are seen at a distance, such as waterfowl on the other side of a large lake or perhaps a hawk on a high cliff, something more powerful is needed. Especially useful is a telescope mounted on a tripod. The scope should range anywhere from 10 to 20 power and, preferably, should have a zoom lens for quick results. The higher the power, the lesser amount of light is available. Therefore, anything stronger than 20 power is not recommended. Furthermore, the objective may be blurred because of heat haze or merely less light, causing less sharpness.

Also necessary is a lightweight tripod on which to mount the telescope. Be sure that the legs have clamps to press down, which will make them more secure. *Never* buy a tripod that has leg screws. Sand and grit will get into the threads, and constant loosening and tightening will cause the joints to become threadbare.

Glossary

BARRED—lengthwise *horizontal* markings, as in tails of many hawks
BREEDING—spring, summer
FACIAL DISK—rounded front part of face, as in owls
FRONTAL SHIELD—bare covering at base of bill, as in gallinules
HEAD TUFT—clump of feathers on top of head, as in some owls
LORE—space between bill and eye
MANDIBLES—upper and lower bills
MEDIAN LINE—stripe through center of crown
NAPE—back of neck
NONBREEDING—fall, winter
PRIMARIES—flight feathers
RECTRICES—tail feathers
RUMP—lower back just above tail
SECONDARIES—wing feathers behind primaries
SPECTACLE—eye ring, plus connecting streak through lore
STREAKED—lengthwise *vertical* markings, as in many sparrows
TARSUS—leg
VENT—undertail coverts

Species Index

English Name	Scientific Name	
Avocet, American	*Recurvirostra americana*	104
Baldplate	*Anas americana*	82
Bittern, American	*Botaurus lentiginosus*	102
Bittern, Least	*Ixobrychus exilis*	102
Blackbird, Brewer's	*Euphagus cyanocephalus*	48
Blackbird, Red-winged	*Agelaius phoeniceus*	46
Blackbird, Yellow-headed	*Xanthocephalus xanthocephalus*	46
Bluebird, Mountain	*Sialia currucoides*	30
Bluebird, Western	*Sialia mexicana*	30
Bobolink	*Dolichonyx oryzivorus*	46
Bobwhite	*Colinus virginianus*	64
Brant	*Branta bernicla*	80
Bufflehead	*Bucephala albeola*	88
Bunting, Indigo	*Passerina cyanea*	30
Bunting, Lark	*Calamospiza melanocorys*	46
Bunting, Lazuli	*Passerina amoena*	30
Bunting, Painted	*Passerina ciris*	30
Bunting, Snow	*Plectrophenax nivalis*	44
Bunting, Varied	*Passerina versicolor*	30
Bushtit	*Psaltriparus minimus*	26
Canvasback	*Aythya valisineria*	86
Cardinal	*Cardinalis cardinalis*	12
Catbird, Gray	*Dumetella carolinensis*	24
Chat, Yellow-breasted	*Icteria virens*	16
Chickadee, Black-capped	*Parus atricapillus*	26
Chickadee, Chestnut-backed	*Parus rufescens*	26
Chickadee, Mountain	*Parus gambeli*	26
Coot, American	*Fulica americana*	96
Cormorant, Brandt's	*Phalacrocorax penicillatus*	98
Cormorant, Double-crested	*Phalacrocorax auritus*	98
Cormorant, Pelagic	*Phalacrocorax pelagicus*	98
Cowbird, Bronzed	*Molothrus aeneus*	48
Cowbird, Brown-headed	*Molothrus ater*	46
Cowbird, Red-eyed	*Molothrus aeneus*	48
Crane, Sandhill	*Grus canadensis*	100
Creeper, Brown	*Certhia familiaris*	50

Crossbill, Red	*Loxia curvirostra*	10
Crossbill, White-winged	*Loxia leucoptera*	10
Crow, American	*Corvus brachyrhynchos*	48
Cuckoo, Yellow-billed	*Coccyzus americanus*	62
Curlew, Long-billed	*Numenius americanus*	104
Dickcissel	*Spiza americana*	44
Dipper	*Cinclus mexicanus*	24
Dove, Ground	*Columbina passerina*	62
Dove, Inca	*Columbina inca*	62
Dove, Mourning	*Zenaida macroura*	62
Dove, Spotted	*Streptopelia chinensis*	62
Dove, White-winged	*Zenaida asiatica*	62
Dowitcher, Long-billed	*Limnodromus scolopaceus*	106
Duck, Black-bellied Whistling	*Dendrocygna autumnalis*	82
Duck, Fulvous Whistling	*Dendrocygna bicolor*	82
Duck, Harlequin	*Histrionicus histrionicus*	90
Duck, Ring-necked	*Aythya collaris*	86
Duck, Ruddy	*Oxyura jamaicensis*	90
Duck, Wood	*Aix sponsa*	84
Dunlin	*Calidris alpina*	108
Eagle, Bald	*Haliaeetus leucocephalus*	68
Eagle, Golden	*Aquila chrysaetos*	68
Egret, Cattle	*Bubulcus ibis*	100
Egret, Great	*Egretta alba*	100
Egret, Snowy	*Egretta thula*	100
Falcon, Peregrine	*Falco peregrinus*	74
Falcon, Prairie	*Falco mexicanus*	74
Finch, House	*Carpodacus mexicanus*	10
Finch, Purple	*Carpodacus purpureus*	10
Finch, Rosy	*Leucosticte arctoa*	10
Flicker, Northern	*Colaptes auratus*	52
Flycatcher, Ash-throated	*Myiarchus cinerascens*	22
Flycatcher, Olive-sided	*Contopus borealis*	22
Flycatcher, Scissor-tailed	*Tyrannus forficatus*	24
Flycatcher, Vermilion	*Pyrocephalus rubinus*	12
Flycatcher, Western	*Empidonax difficilis*	22
Gadwall	*Anas strepera*	82
Gallinule, Common (Moorhen)	*Gallinula chloropus*	96
Gnatcatcher, Black-tailed	*Polioptila melanura*	26
Gnatcatcher, Blue-gray	*Polioptila caerulea*	26
Godwit, Marbled	*Limosa fedoa*	104
Goldeneye, Barrow's	*Bucephala islandica*	88
Goldeneye, Common	*Bucephala clangula*	88

Goldfinch, American	*Carduelis tristis*	14
Goldfinch, Lesser (Dark-backed)	*Carduelis psaltria*	14
Goldfinch, Lawrence's	*Carduelis lawrencei*	14
Goose, Canada	*Branta canadensis*	80
Goose, Snow	*Anser caerulescens*	80
Goose, White-fronted	*Anser albifrons*	80
Goshawk, Northern	*Accipiter gentilis*	72
Grackle, Common	*Quiscalus quiscula*	48
Grackle, Great-tailed	*Quiscalus mexicanus*	48
Grebe, Clark's	*Aechmophorus clarkii*	94
Grebe, Eared	*Podiceps nigricollis*	94
Grebe, Horned	*Podiceps auritus*	94
Grebe, Pied-billed	*Podilymbus podiceps*	94
Grebe, Western	*Aechmophorus occidentalis*	94
Grosbeak, Black-headed	*Pheucticus melanocephalus*	14
Grosbeak, Blue	*Passerina caerulea*	30
Grosbeak, Evening	*Coccothraustes vespertinus*	14
Grosbeak, Pine	*Pinicola enucleator*	10
Grouse, Blue	*Dendragapus obscurus*	66
Grouse, Ruffed	*Bonasa umbellus*	66
Grouse, Sage	*Centrocercus urophasianus*	66
Grouse, Sharp-tailed	*Pedioecetes phasianellus*	66
Guillemot, Pigeon	*Cepphus columba*	92
Gull, Bonaparte's	*Larus philadelphia*	116
Gull, California	*Larus californicus*	114
Gull, Franklin's	*Larus pipixcan*	116
Gull, Glaucous-winged	*Larus glaucescens*	114
Gull, Heermann's	*Larus heermanni*	114
Gull, Herring	*Larus argentatus*	114
Gull, Mew	*Larus canus*	114
Gull, Ring-billed	*Larus delawarensis*	114
Gull, Western	*Larus occidentalis*	114
Harrier, Northern	*Circus cyaneus*	72
Hawk, Ferruginous	*Buteo regalis*	70
Hawk, Marsh	*Circus cyaneus*	72
Hawk, Red-shouldered	*Buteo lineatus*	70
Hawk, Red-tailed	*Buteo jamaicensis*	70
Hawk, Rough-legged	*Buteo lagopus*	70
Hawk, Sharp-shinned	*Accipiter striatus*	12
Hawk, Swainson's	*Buteo swainsoni*	70
Heron, Black-crowned Night	*Nycticorax nycticorax*	102
Heron, Great Blue	*Ardea herodias*	100
Heron, Green-backed	*Butorides striatus*	102
Hummingbird, Allen's	*Selasphorus sasin*	60
Hummingbird, Anna's	*Calypte anna*	60
Hummingbird, Black-chinned	*Archilochus alexandri*	60
Hummingbird, Broad-billed	*Cynanthus latirostris*	60

Hummingbird, Broad-tailed	*Selasphorus platycercus*	60
Hummingbird, Calliope	*Stellula calliope*	60
Hummingbird, Costa's	*Calypte costae*	60
Hummingbird, Rufous	*Selasphorus rufus*	60
Ibis, White-faced	*Plegadis chihi*	102
Jay, Blue	*Cyanocitta cristata*	28
Jay, Gray	*Perisoreus canadensis*	24
Jay, Pinyon	*Gymnorhinus cyanocephalus*	28
Jay, Scrub	*Aphelocoma coerulescens*	28
Jay, Steller's	*Cyanocitta stelleri*	28
Junco, Dark-eyed	*Junco hyemalis*	32
Kestrel, American	*Falco sparverius*	74
Killdeer	*Charadrius vociferus*	112
Kingbird, Eastern	*Tyrannus tyrannus*	22
Kingbird, Western	*Tyrannus verticalis*	22
Kingfisher, Belted	*Ceryle alcyon*	28
Kinglet, Golden-crowned	*Regulus satrapa*	20
Kinglet, Ruby-crowned	*Regulus calendula*	20
Kite, Black-shouldered	*Elanus caeruleus*	74
Kite, Mississippi	*Ictinia mississippiensis*	74
Knot, Red	*Calidris canutus*	108
Lark, Horned	*Eremophila alpestris*	44
Longspur, Chestnut-collared	*Calcarius ornatus*	44
Longspur, Lapland	*Calcarius lapponicus*	44
Loon, Arctic (Pacific)	*Gavia arctica/pacifica*	92
Loon, Common	*Gavia immer*	92
Loon, Red-throated	*Gavia stellata*	92
Magpie, Black-billed	*Pica pica*	48
Mallard	*Anas platyrhynchos*	82
Martin, Purple	*Progne subis*	56
Meadowlark, Western	*Sturnella neglecta*	44
Merganser, Common	*Mergus merganser*	88
Merganser, Hooded	*Mergus cucullatus*	88
Merganser, Red-breasted	*Mergus serrator*	88
Merlin	*Falco columbarius*	74
Mockingbird, Northern	*Mimus polyglottos*	24
Murre, Thin-billed (Common)	*Uria aalge*	92
Nighthawk, Common	*Chordeiles minor*	58
Nutcracker, Clark's	*Nucifraga columbiana*	24
Nuthatch, Pygmy	*Sitta pygmaea*	50
Nuthatch, Red-breasted	*Sitta canadensis*	50
Nuthatch, White-breasted	*Sitta carolinensis*	50

Oriole, Northern ("Bullock's")	*Icterus galbula*	12
Oriole, Hooded	*Icterus cucullatus*	12
Oriole, Scott's	*Icterus parisorum*	14
Osprey	*Pandion haliaetus*	72
Owl, Barn	*Tyto alba*	78
Owl, Burrowing	*Athene cunicularia*	76
Owl, Elf	*Micrathene whitneyi*	76
Owl, Great Horned	*Bubo virginianus*	78
Owl, Long-eared	*Asio otus*	78
Owl, Northern Pygmy	*Glaucidium gnoma*	76
Owl, Saw-whet	*Aegolius acadicus*	76
Owl, Short-eared	*Asio flammeus*	78
Owl, Spotted	*Strix occidentalis*	78
Owl, Western Screech	*Otus kennicottii*	76
Oystercatcher, Black	*Haematopus bachmani*	110
Partridge, Chukar	*Alectoris graeca*	64
Partridge, Gray	*Perdix perdix*	64
Pelican, Brown	*Pelecanus occidentalis*	98
Pelican, White	*Pelecanus erythrorhynchos*	98
Pewee, Western Wood	*Contopus sordidulus*	22
Phainopepla	*Phainopepla nitens*	46
Phalarope, Red-necked	*Phalaropus lobatus*	108
Phalarope, Wilson's	*Phalaropus tricolor*	108
Pheasant, Ring-necked	*Phasianus colchicus*	66
Phoebe, Black	*Sayornis nigricans*	22
Phoebe, Say's	*Sayornis saya*	22
Pigeon, Band-tailed	*Columba fasciata*	62
Pigeon, Rock (Domestic)	*Columba livia*	62
Pintail	*Anas acuta*	82
Pipit, Water	*Anthus spinoletta*	44
Plover, Black-bellied	*Pluvialis squatarola*	112
Plover, Golden	*Pluvialis dominica*	112
Plover, Mountain	*Charadrius montanus*	112
Plover, Semipalmated	*Charadrius semipalmatus*	112
Plover, Snowy	*Charadrius alexandrinus*	112
Poorwill	*Phalaenoptilus nuttallii*	58
Pyrrhuloxia	*Cardinalis sinuatus*	12
Quail, California	*Callipepla californica*	64
Quail, Gambel's	*Callipepla gambelii*	64
Quail, Mountain	*Oreortyx pictus*	64
Quail, Scaled	*Callipepla squamata*	64
Rail, Clapper	*Rallus longirostris*	96
Rail, King	*Rallus elegans*	96
Rail, Virginia	*Rallus limicola*	96
Raven, Northern	*Corvus corax*	48
Redhead	*Aythya americana*	86

Redstart, American	*Setophaga ruticilla*	18
Redstart, Painted	*Myioborus pictus*	18
Roadrunner	*Geococcyx californianus*	66
Robin, American	*Turdus migratorius*	42
Sanderling	*Calidris alba*	108
Sandpiper, Least	*Calidris minutilla*	108
Sandpiper, Rock	*Calidris ptilocnemis*	110
Sandpiper, Spotted	*Actitis macularia*	106
Sandpiper, Upland	*Bartramia longicauda*	106
Sandpiper, Western	*Calidris mauri*	108
Sapsucker, Red-breasted	*Sphyrapicus ruber*	52
Sapsucker, Williamson's	*Sphyrapicus thyroideus*	52
Sapsucker, Yellow-bellied	*Sphyrapicus varius*	52
Scaup, Greater	*Aythya marila*	86
Scaup, Lesser	*Aythya affinis*	86
Scoter, Black	*Melanitta nigra*	90
Scoter, Surf	*Melanitta perspicillata*	90
Scoter, White-winged	*Melanitta fusca*	90
Shoveler	*Anas clypeata*	84
Shrike, Loggerhead	*Lanius ludovicianus*	24
Siskin, Pine	*Carduelis pinus*	14
Snipe, Common	*Gallinago gallinago*	106
Solitaire, Townsend's	*Myadestes townsendi*	24
Sora	*Porzana carolina*	96
Sparrow, Black-chinned	*Spizella atrogularis*	32
Sparrow, Black-throated	*Amphispiza bilineata*	32
Sparrow, Chipping	*Spizella passerina*	36
Sparrow, Fox	*Passerella iliaca*	36
Sparrow, Golden-crowned	*Zonotrichia atricapilla*	34
Sparrow, Harris'	*Zonotrichia querula*	34
Sparrow, House	*Passer domesticus*	34
Sparrow, Lark	*Chondestes grammacus*	34
Sparrow, Rufous-crowned	*Aimophila ruficeps*	36
Sparrow, Sage	*Amphispiza belli*	32
Sparrow, Savannah	*Passerculus sandwichensis*	36
Sparrow, Song	*Melospiza melodia*	36
Sparrow, Tree	*Spizella arborea*	36
Sparrow, Vesper	*Pooecetes gramineus*	36
Sparrow, White-crowned	*Zonotrichia leucophrys*	34
Sparrow, White-throated	*Zonotrichia albicollis*	34
Starling	*Sturnus vulgaris*	46
Stilt, Black-necked	*Himantopus mexicanus*	104
Surfbird	*Aphriza virgata*	110
Swallow, Bank	*Riparia riparia*	56
Swallow, Barn	*Hirundo rustica*	56
Swallow, Cliff	*Hirundo pyrrhonota*	56
Swallow, Rough-winged	*Stelgidopteryx serripennis*	56
Swallow, Tree	*Tachycineta bicolor*	56

Swallow, Violet-green	*Tachycineta thalassina*	56
Swan, Tundra (Whistling)	*Cygnus columbianus*	80
Swan, Trumpeter	*Cygnus buccinator*	80
Swift, Black	*Cypseloides niger*	58
Swift, Vaux's	*Chaetura vauxi*	58
Swift, White-throated	*Aeronautes saxatalis*	58
Tanager, Hepatic	*Piranga flava*	12
Tanager, Summer	*Piranga rubra*	12
Tanager, Western	*Piranga ludoviciana*	14
Tattler, Wandering	*Tringa incana*	110
Teal, Blue-winged	*Anas discors*	84
Teal, Cinnamon	*Anas cyanoptera*	84
Teal, Green-winged	*Anas crecca*	84
Tern, Black	*Chlidonias niger*	116
Tern, Caspian	*Sterna caspia*	116
Tern, Elegant	*Sterna elegans*	116
Tern, Forster's	*Sterna forsteri*	116
Tern, Least	*Sterna antillarum*	116
Thrasher, Bendire's	*Toxostoma bendirei*	40
Thrasher, California	*Toxostoma redivivum*	40
Thrasher, Curve-billed	*Toxostoma curvirostre*	40
Thrasher, Sage	*Oreoscoptes montanus*	40
Thrush, Hermit	*Catharus guttatus*	42
Thrush, Swainson's	*Catharus ustulatus*	42
Thrush, Varied	*Ixoreus naevius*	42
Tit, Yellow-headed	*Auriparus flaviceps*	26
Titmouse, Bridled	*Parus wollweberi*	26
Titmouse, Plain	*Parus inornatus*	26
Towhee, Abert's	*Pipilo aberti*	40
Towhee, Brown	*Pipilo fuscus*	40
Towhee, Green-tailed	*Pipilo chlorurus*	40
Towhee, Rufous-sided ("Spotted")	*Pipilo erythrophthalmus*	40
Turkey, Wild	*Meleagris gallopavo*	66
Turnstone, Black	*Arenaria melanocephala*	110
Turnstone, Ruddy	*Arenaria interpres*	110
Veery	*Catharus fuscescens*	42
Verdin (Yellow-headed Tit)	*Auriparus flaviceps*	26
Vireo, Gray	*Vireo vicinior*	20
Vireo, Red-eyed	*Vireo olivaceus*	20
Vireo, Solitary	*Vireo solitarius*	20
Vireo, Warbling	*Vireo gilvus*	20
Vulture, Black	*Coragyps atratus*	68
Vulture, Turkey	*Cathartes aura*	68
Warbler, Black-throated Gray	*Dendroica nigrescens*	18
Warbler, Grace's	*Dendroica graciae*	18

About the Authors and Artist

JOHN BULL, a leading authority on birds, has been on the staff of the Ornithology Department of the American Museum of Natural History since 1962. He is co-author of *Birds of North America: Eastern Region,* and the bestselling *The Audubon Society Field Guide to North American Birds, Eastern Region.* He lives in New York City with his wife, Edith.

EDITH BULL majored in zoology at Skidmore College and received an M.A. in Vertebrate Paleontology from Columbia University. She has worked in the Department of Vertebrate Paleontology at the American Museum of Natural History and has also conducted classes for children in the Education Department of the Museum.

JAMES COE is a noted naturalist and artist whose most recent works include *Birds of New Guinea* and *The Audubon Master Guide to Birding.* His illustrations have been featured in *Animal Kingdom* and *American Birds* magazines. He lives in Hannacroix, New York.

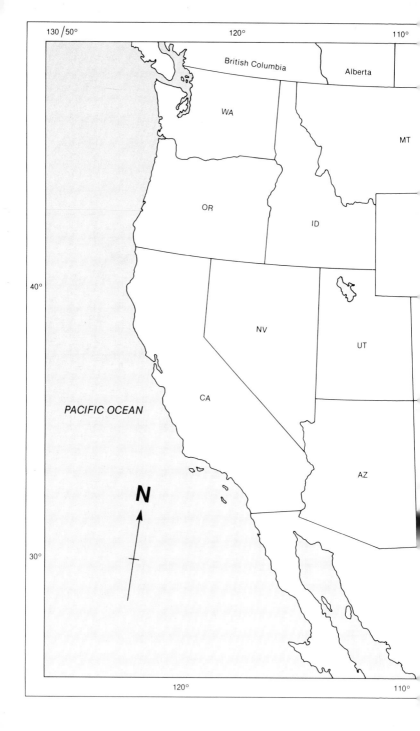